TUPAC REMEMBERED

Page 165 constitutes a continuation of the copyright page.

Library of Congress Cataloging-in-Publication Data is available.

ISBN: 978-1-932855-76-0

Tupac Remembered: Bearing Witness to a Life and Legacy
is produced by becker&mayer! LLC, Bellevue, Washington
www.beckermayer.com.

Produced under license from becker&mayer! and Amaru Entertainment, Inc.

Design: Joanna Price
Editorial: Jenna Land Free
Image Research: Shayna Ian
Production Coordinator: Leah Finger

Amaru Legal and Business Affairs: Dina LaPolt, LaPolt Law, P.C.
Amaru General Counsel: Donald David, Esq.
Amaru Publicity: Versa Manos, Gorgeouspr.com

Front cover photo: © Reisig & Taylor Photography

MANUFACTURED IN CHINA

10 9 8 7 6 5 4 3 2 1

Chronicle Books LLC
680 Second Street
San Francisco, CA 94107

www.chroniclebooks.com

TUPAC REMEMBERED

bearing witness to a life and legacy

EDITED BY MOLLY MONJAUZE
WITH GLORIA COX & STACI ROBINSON

CHRONICLE BOOKS
SAN FRANCISCO

Sekyiwa and Tupac.

FOR SEKYIWA

As a little girl, she inspired the man who in turn became the inspiration for an entire generation. All grown

up, she is now the woman I call when I need advice on how to be a better mother, a better friend, a better

human being; and with every answer she gives me, I think about how lucky Tupac was to have such an

extraordinary sister.

At the video shoot for "All Bout You."

CONTENTS

INTRODUCTION

I have thought about a project like this many times in the last eleven years. The first time was just a couple days after Tupac died. I was at Jasmine Guy's house. Jada Pinkett was there, Tupac's girlfriend was there, Yaasmyn Fula (Yaki Kadafi's mother) was there, and I think his first manager, Leila Steinberg, was there. We were all sitting in the living room having our own conversations about what we were feeling. None of us were really connecting to what the other was saying; we were angry and brokenhearted, we were confused and trying desperately to make sense of what had just occurred. The reason we were there was to talk about how we could be of help to Afeni, but that's not what we were talking about. We were babbling about how unreal it was that something like this could happen, what went wrong, who could have done this, why would someone have done this, for what?

It was Jasmine and Jada who brought us back to what we were there for. They started talking about how Afeni had to get an attorney, how she had to be very careful and ready for everyone making claims to Tupac's estate. I was Tupac's assistant when he was killed and had no intention of leaving Afeni at this time or any time after, and was taking notes on what Jasmine and Jada were saying needed to be done. Somewhere in between listening to the words coming from this circle of women, and watching the tears running down their faces, it occurred to me that if you lined all of us up, one of us was probably present at some point in the story of Tupac's life.

As Jada was dictating to me what I should tell Afeni she must do to protect herself and his estate, I looked at her and remembered all the times Tupac would tell me about his best friend from Baltimore, and how they were going to be famous actors together, and how much he loved her and missed her.

I thought about Leila, and the first time he told me about this lady in Santa Rosa who was going to be his manager, and exactly how he planned for her to get him through doors that wouldn't open so quickly if it was him they saw in front. I thought about how I used to call her house for him when he was sleeping on her couch a million years ago, and the adventures he would tell me about having on tour with Digital Underground after Leila brought Tupac to Atron Gregory and made that "Shock G connection."

I looked at Jasmine and thought about how grateful I was to her for being that safe haven for him to go to after he was shot the first time in New York. When he was at his lowest point, and felt most betrayed, it was Jasmine he turned to, it was she who opened her home up to him and his family with no agenda except to be there for her friend.

I looked at his girlfriend, who was brokenhearted, and thought about the many conversations Tupac and I had had in the last couple months about his future plans, about building a family, and how he had reached a point where he'd felt hopeful about what was to come.

I saw Yaasmyn, who just a week and a half earlier, the night of September 7, was at my house rocking Tupac's niece Imani to sleep on my back porch, telling me how Tupac used to like to be rocked to sleep when he was Imani's age.

I turned to myself and thought about the first night I saw him after he had been released from prison, how much fun we had laughing about nothing, remembering the times years earlier when we'd stayed up all night listening to rock albums—David Bowie, Pink Floyd—nights when he'd tell me which songs he planned on sampling once he got a deal.

I thought to myself, "If all the women in this room ever had to tell his life story, I think we could come pretty close, just sharing our memories."

During his last year, I would walk into the house and he would yell, "I love you . . . because you will never go to the *National Enquirer*," and start laughing. He told me he loved me because I always believed in him and because he trusted me. What he didn't know was that it was impossible *not* to believe in him. I never heard him say he was going to do something and not know without a shadow of a doubt that it was going to happen. I thought anybody who didn't see what he was capable of was blind. I never understood anyone's surprise in his success—I'd think to myself, "Do they really not get it?" I have a similar feeling when people meet Afeni for the first time and are blown away. They look at me and say, "My God, I had no idea. She is amazing. I have never met a woman like her before in my life." I say the same thing every time: "Where do you think Tupac came from? He is his mother's son, what were you expecting, exactly?"

Putting this book together reminded me of how many people Tupac connected with. I am not a poet, an actor, a revolutionary, a musician, a rapper, a politician, a gangster, a comedian, a music mogul or a scholar, yet he connected with me in addition to all of these individuals. Tupac loved every person for who they were, and for not trying to be anything different. He used to say to me that every single person in our lives represented a piece of a puzzle, some of us may have been bigger than the other parts, but without even one of the smallest pieces, the puzzle would be incomplete. Tupac is our common denominator. He has become what all of us have in common with each other. For many of us, he has become a source of motivation we share.

In addition to knowing what he would accomplish, Tupac could see in his friends what we couldn't even see in ourselves. Do you think it's a coincidence that Tupac and Leila wrote poetry together, read books and discussed starting a non-profit to help children together—and that's exactly what Leila does today? Do you think it's an accident that in high school, Tupac and Jada would talk about becoming famous actors one day—and they both did? In the late '80s, Tupac made plans for me to write about him once he got a deal. I didn't even know I enjoyed writing then, yet here I sit, over fifteen years later, writing about Tupac Amaru Shakur just like he said I was supposed to.

In the last eleven years, I've worked on many projects Tupac's mother has put out; with each new project, the idea for this book would come up again. I'd always say after we finished an album, "I wish we had a camera rolling while we made this album, nobody would believe what happens." What happens is that we sit in the studio and each person who comes in to do a verse or a track also brings what I refer to as their "Tupac story."

During the production of *Pac's Life*, I brought the book we had just finished, *Tupac Shakur Legacy*, into the studio so everyone could look at it. Snoop and his crew were in one studio, LT Hutton, Kurupt, and Daz were in another, and I was going from room to room. LT, Daz, and Kurupt were looking at the book and saw a photo of themselves, and they started talking about the day the photo was taken. LT started talking about Tupac, imitating his George Jefferson walk, making fun of him, the way only one of his friends could, while Kurupt and Daz were laughing at the photo. Snoop, meanwhile, was giving me direction about the album. I realized that his friends should be telling these stories, and that a straightforward biography would never be able to give these details the way an essay book would.

Every chapter reminds me of something I love about him, something I miss about him, something that drove me nuts about him. This book could have been a thousand pages long with five hundred different interviews and there would still have been something different in each one. These stories help me when I am missing him and can't make sense of him not being here. When I read the chapters from the people who never even met Tupac, but are so affected by him they are out there helping others because he helped them . . . I really get it.

When he was first murdered, I did not want to go outside. I was convinced the world had gone mad. I kept thinking, do they know who they took? Do they realize the damage they have done? Who will care for people nobody else cared for? Who will step up now that they have taken him and call people out when no one else will? I thought, this is how people felt when Dr. King was murdered. This is what it felt like when Malcolm was taken. Now who will be our leader? I never heard anybody else in our generation talk about helping those in need like he used to, I never knew anyone so affected by what they saw on the news like Tupac was.

I remember once we were watching a story on TV about a thirteen-year-old girl who had been gang-raped, left in an abandoned house with the door hammered shut, and set on fire by a group of very young teenage boys. I remember being horrified at what I was hearing and saying, "What kind of animals would do such a thing?" Tupac looked at me with tears in his eyes and said, "Imagine what kind of animal hurt a child so badly, it caused them to do something like that." It's what he always used to do. Tupac saw past what the rest of us were so quick to pass judgment on. He searched for the true cause of an issue, not what was on the surface. He says it in his poem, "The Rose That Grew from Concrete," when he tells us all to celebrate the rose that, against all odds, had grown from a crack in the concrete. He used to say that instead of judging it because of its bent branches and less-than-perfect petals, we should be in shock that it was strong enough to even find the will to grow in such an unfit place. Tupac took the word NIGGA and decided he had the ability to give it a different meaning. He made the letters stand for Never Ignorant Getting Goals Accomplished. This was when he was nineteen, long before any Oprah special on the "N" word. I get so frustrated when I see these shows, because he would be the first one on the panel exposing the *real* problems, and the first to offer his help in solving them.

As I read through the chapters of this book and laugh and cry, I am reminded of all the many reasons I miss my friend.

I feel his absence whenever one of the kids graduates, or has an issue he would be the first to lecture them about. I miss him every time his sister accomplishes anything he would be proud of her for, and every time one of the Outlawz becomes a father again. It drives me crazy every time I see something being done he was talking about doing *eleven* years ago and people think it's so original now. I want him here every time someone refers to him as a legend. It reminds me of one of my favorite daily arguments he and I used to have, and there were a lot to choose from. He used to stand in front of me, usually in his boxers, cross his arms, and say with his head tilted, "You know you work for a living legend, right?" This would always incite me to tell him to get over himself, and we'd go back and forth for hours. I think one of the reasons he liked me around was to have someone to argue with. I think it kept him grounded to have people with him who didn't care if he was a rap star, who didn't think any differently of him if he didn't sell a million albums.

One of Tupac's favorite things to do was to give gifts. It didn't matter if he knew you or what form the gift came in, he just got so much pleasure from the act of giving (another quality he and his mother have in common). One day he must have thought I could use a pick-me-up, and he told me that I could have anything I wanted. We could jump on a plane and go to Paris to have dinner and go shopping if I felt like it—whatever I could name I could have. I told him first, to stop showing off, and second, that all I wanted was for him not to let any of this fame change him. I made him actually promise this out loud. I don't really think he was showing off, I would just say that stuff to make him laugh. Sometimes it worked, sometimes he would just fire me. I believe that ultimately, he wanted the same thing from all of us—his friends, his family, even his fans—he didn't want *us* to change because of his fame, he wanted us to let him be the imperfect person he was the first to claim to be.

This book is made up of memories and stories from a group of individuals who let him be who he really was; we didn't turn our backs on him on his bad days, we didn't have hidden agendas or look at him any differently if he was successful or not. This book is made up of heartfelt moments that were shared between Tupac and people who were very important to him. They are honest and funny, some are sad and thought-provoking, and in true Tupac form, very entertaining.

This is a book that every time I need to be reminded of how good we are all capable of being, I will pick up to read.

—Molly Monjauze

A CHILD
AT WAR

"To really understand Pac, you have to understand the Panther movement. The movement was purposely destroyed, and a lot of the Panthers' families' lives were destroyed. It didn't just hit adults, but also children. Pac was one of those children. He was coming up out of a movement that was so dedicated and so strong, but lost. And in a lot of instances, in any war or tragedy, the people everyone talks about least, and last, are the children. People who were friends weren't friends no more. A lot of people went to jail. A lot of people died, or were murdered. A lot of people just went crazy. And he was left to deal with that, as were most of the kids in the Panthers. That's what Pac represented. It's true he represented the best in human potential, but he also represented a child at war; a child who grew into a man.

"Coming from those circumstances, how much different would any of us be? How would we have grown up? Would we even have gotten as far as Pac did?"

—MOS DEF

SEKYIWA SHAKUR

> Tupac and his sister Sekyiwa, or "Set," shared a relationship filled with sibling banter and love, which grew into one of protection and pride as they became adults. They moved often throughout their childhood, going from New York to Baltimore to Marin City. The constant they had was one another.

From the time I was still waddling in Pampers, I would cry when our cousins picked on Tupac and teased him. And then Tupac would yell at me for crying and making him look like a punk. Then our cousins would tease him even more because I was crying. When I turned five and Tupac was around nine, we'd play with all our cousins, but Tupac always wanted to kick me to the side. He was very protective of me when we were playing outside, very strict about not getting into problems with other people. My mom used to tell us that a woman's mouth could get a black man killed, so we were always concerned and cautious about that. I was supposed to be careful about not getting him in trouble.

Growing up with all of the parents, not just Afeni, but all of the parents we had, was hard. If we'd been different people, I don't know if we'd have been able to survive like we did. If I'd grown up with anyone else besides Tupac as my brother, I don't think I would be the person that I am. If he'd grown up with anyone else as his sister, I don't know if he'd have become the person he was.

When we lived at 92 Morningside in Harlem, Tupac and I shared a room. We had single beds, side-by-side. Tupac would always fall asleep listening to music. He listened to James Ingram's "Just Once" a lot. I'd fall asleep with my dolls. I had around ten doll babies, and each night I'd rotate who got to lie next to me. I didn't want any of them to think that I loved them more than the other. I'd pray, and one of my prayers was that we'd all die at a family reunion, 'cause I didn't want anyone to die first and miss everyone. Because we grew up in this post-Vietnam era, and were, as they said, at war with the Pigs, Tupac and I grew up with warped states of mind. He'd cry himself to sleep a lot . . . always listening to music.

We had lots of books. One in particular I remember was the children's version of *The Autobiography of Malcolm X*. Tupac had a Rubik's Cube he mastered. He loved *Star Wars* back then. He also made a lot of homemade toys.

Tupac and Sekyiwa sit on the lap of Geronimo Jijaga (Pratt) in a family photo. Afeni is standing in blue.

One time I had a loose tooth and Tupac wanted to pull it out. I was crying and crying, saying, "No, Tupac. You can't pull out my tooth." Then he started crying. "You don't trust me. I'm your brother and you don't love me." We were two very dramatic children. So we were all drama-ized and running around the house and crying and having a big fight. He tried to corner me, and I ran from him, and we ended up wrestling on the kitchen floor. So I got this bottle of soy sauce I knew he wanted to drink out of the refrigerator and I said, "I'm gonna drink this now." I was being spiteful. I put it in my mouth, and he smacked it out of my hand, and when he did, my tooth came out. This was a typical scenario for us, the simplest thing turned into the biggest drama.

In Baltimore, we needed each other more than ever. We didn't even have to fake the drama because the real life had enough. When Tupac and I woke up in the morning, there wouldn't be anything to eat for breakfast. We were poor. We got food stamps once a month, and we'd clean the house the days that my mom would leave to go get them. One time, when I was busy cleaning up the kitchen, Tupac yelled, "SETCHI! COME HERE!" I ran over, and saw a rat stuck in this rat hole. The rat was so big that it couldn't get through. When my mother got home she was mad we didn't finish cleaning so we showed her the rat. We sealed the food away, but by nighttime, we started to hear rats running through the cabinets. We'd hear, "thump, thump, thump" all night long. By day three, we had no food left. Every month this would happen. And we'd have to wait a few weeks until we got food stamps again.

The summer before he died I came out to L.A. from Atlanta. I had just spent the last two months doing things for myself, looking better, feeling better. I learned to drive, went to hair school, lost a whole bunch of weight, and totally went through a transformation. When I got to Pac's, he opened the door and couldn't believe it. He was so happy to see me. He was tickling me, pinching my cheeks, grabbing my earlobes, and chasing me around the living room. He was so proud of me. We talked like we hadn't talked in years. He had recently heard that our mom had seen a family friend that was rumored to still be on drugs. He asked, "Set, do you think Mom is using again?" First it shocked me, because he hadn't been around enough to know she hadn't . . . 'cause it was clear my mother hadn't. But at the same time, it was refreshing to have those brother/sister talks. It was good to know that I was still the one he'd come to. We hadn't had a talk like that in years.

When my mom, my kids, and I were leaving for the airport to go back to Atlanta, we stopped by his house to see him and say good-bye. My mom went up to the house and I waited inside the limo with the kids. He came back out with my mom, and leaned in and smiled at me. He said, "I just wanted to let you know how proud I am of you. I wanted to say sorry for all the times I left you. I know I made a lot of mistakes in Marin City. I should've been there for you more. I'm so proud of you. You're beautiful. I know you wanna be independent and you wanna be a strong black woman. And I know you wanna do this hair stuff. But you have something that I don't have. You have your kids. I want you to spend more time with the kids. I am gonna make sure you're okay. I'm gonna make sure you have what you need. I forgive you for everything that went on and I hope you forgive me. I love you." He was saying stuff he hadn't said in years. It was like he was saying good-bye.

People always assumed that I felt a weight on my shoulders about Tupac's success. If I felt a weight about anything growing up, it was because he was cuter than me. Tupac was already a celebrity to me by the time I was three. But I have to say that I am completely in awe of the fact that he became what he was supposed to be when he grew up. And when I look at that in a universal way, I think, "Wow, am I doing what I am supposed to be doing now that I'm grown up?" My nuclear family, which included my mother, my father, and my brother, all changed the world by the time they were twenty-five. I'm thirty-one and I just learned how to make banana pudding.

Tupac trying to teach Sekyiwa's son, Malik, how to crawl.

MUTULU SHAKUR

> Mutulu Shakur, a member of the New Afrikan Independence Movement, was Tupac's stepfather. Though he was incarcerated for most of Tupac's life, he was still able to share advice, wisdom, and life lessons. Mutulu was instrumental in assisting Tupac substantiate the Thug Life movement in the early 1990s. Thug Life became an honor code and celebration of the street soldiers Tupac worked hard to represent. But of all of Mutulu's contributions to Tupac's life, the most important was his last name.

Tupac was specifically a revolutionary rapper. Not the revolution of the 1960s or the 1970s, but a revolutionary rapper of his time. You may or may not praise the fact that Tupac had a political history, but I think it's important that people understand the post-traumatic stress associated with that history. It's important that people understand his connection to his heritage and that this heritage is part of the liberation struggle. It's also important to understand it's never been easy. It wasn't easy for me not to be with him, to give up my life for the struggle and for my family. It's a natural thing for children who are away from their fathers to be aggravated, to be mad.

Tupac and I had many discussions. During those discussions we began to clarify what struggle is and what is the stress of struggle. We would argue. Tupac and I had beefs. When he tattooed "Thug Life," I asked him, "What is this 'Thug Life'?" I said, "What is that about—snatching someone's pocketbook?" We argued about it. He said, "Hell no, it ain't about snatching a pocketbook!" I told him to define it. To do some research and to make his own definition. I told him I didn't have no problem with it, but to come up with something so that it was clear what he was talking about.

Our relationship was one of struggle and support.

"To My Son"

I love you whenever . . . forever. Tupac, so much I needed to say, so much you wanted to say.
Many conversations between us within the ether, whenever . . . forever.

The pain inflicted that scarred your soul but not your spirit gave force to rebellion.
Many couldn't see your dreams or understand your nightmares. How could they, Tupac?
I knew your love and understood your passion.
But you knew of your beginning and saw your end . . . racing toward it.

You taught and fought through your songs and deeds. RATT-TATT-TATT of words
penetrating the contradiction of your existence. Whenever . . . forever.

Who cares? We cared, Tupac. The Shakurs have been guided by struggle,
prepared or not, whenever . . . forever.

We've exposed our existence, naked from fear, to those who would hear the positive.
Who would witness the stress wear and tear of this lonely path.

You couldn't have evaded the effect or the changes.
You inherited it, it was in your genes.

But still, you danced your dance, you lived your life.
You forced loyalty on those who would fake and shake at the true vision. You were Tupac.

—Mutulu Shakur, written the night of Tupac's death from Mutulu's cell inside
the federal penitentiary in Florence, Colorado, to be read at Tupac's memorial.

JAMALA LESANE

> Tupac and his first cousin Jamala Lesane lived together often throughout their childhood. At the height of his fame, Tupac moved Jamala and her daughter, Imani, into his Los Angeles home—partly because he loved Jamala like the older sister he never had, but also because he refused to eat anyone else's fried chicken.

When we were kids, Tupac was so smart. Even when he was little, he was a smart dude. As the two eldest out of the cousins, we used to compete a lot. Tupac always had to be the boss, no matter what game we were playing. If we were playing school, he had to be the teacher. He would just beat you with his intelligence. Since we were the closest in age, we would argue a lot over who would have the higher position in the game, and because I wasn't good at spelling or pronouncing words properly, he would use that against me and figure out a way to take my position. He would say things like, "I bet you can't spell harpsichord." I'd always be like, "Okay fine . . . you got it."

Tupac and I used to fight all the time—every day. I remember one time in Harlem when we had it out. I had short hair all my life, and I was always sensitive about it. Pac knew about my little complex, and he would use it to tease me. One time when we were playing outside, he said something like, "That's why your hair won't grow." Then he called me baldheaded. That shit used to hurt me. So the only way I knew I could get a sting back at him was to say, "That's why your mother was in jail." Soon we were going back and forth with our insults out in the street. My mother heard about it, and whipped the shit out of both of us.

This fighting went on for years. We got a little older and I still didn't know how to spell harpsichord. And he would still use his charm and intelligence against me. He'd say, "I can do it better, 'cause you're not smart enough," or "you're not bright enough."

Tupac, Afeni, and Sekyiwa were a part of our household. We grew up close-knit. Whether they were up the street, or in the apartment upstairs, we were always basically one household. We had to share everything, even our birthdays were the same month, so we'd always celebrate together. There were a lot of us. Our only income back then was Tom's check [Tupac's uncle]. And his check took care of everybody.

Poverty affected Pac in a big way. He hated being poor. I mean, we were all poor, but he was *poor*. He wasn't gonna let anything stop him from getting what he wanted. He had to build a wall to separate himself from us . . . from his family. He didn't care if the lights were out and niggas was hungry, he was out there and trying to become somebody. He wasn't even gonna let anyone in his family stop him.

Pac's immediate family—never mind the revolutionaries, but us—we were welfare recipients, ghetto, drug dealers, and drug abusers. We were the no-hot-water, no-heat, no-Christmas, doped-up, drugged-out kind of family. Tom was the only one ever working. We were lazy. Sheets hangin' up in the window. Tupac was the only one out of all of us who had the passion to get out there, the only one who could've taken it as far as he took it. He worked hard to get where he was.

I first realized Pac was really somebody, that he was an icon, in '92. Before then, he was just Pac. I was living in Washington Heights in New York, at 179th and St. Nick, and Pac and I went to the store together. This mob of people just started to move toward him, to rush him. At that very moment, I realized, "Dang, Pac, you *are* famous." Fame didn't change him at all, though.

He got all the thug stuff from his mom. They were so much alike. Afeni was a thug too. When Afeni was a black woman in the Panthers, she had more guts than any man in the movement. Men were afraid of her. They feared her intelligence, her boldness, and her heart. And that's what made her a thug. The same with Pac. People didn't fear him because they thought he'd be the first nigga to shoot—they feared him because of his intelligence and his boldness. Pac got it all from his mother. Afeni is a bad muthafucka.

When he bought his house in Calabasas, he was at a point in his life when he wanted to settle down and just chill. When he came home at the end of the day, he wanted kids around. He wanted me and my daughter, Imani, there. He wanted his sister's son and daughter, Malik and Nzhinga, there. He wanted to see spilled milk on the floor and wanted the kids to be running around his backyard. He wanted something to come home to. He needed that for fulfillment in his life. But there's another reason he wanted us around: I was the only one who could make his fried chicken. I'd have to make it for him every day so Molly could come to the house and get it to drive it to him wherever he was. He wouldn't eat anyone else's.

The most important thing my cousin taught me was that you can do and be whatever you want to be in this world. He taught me that you can come from nothing, start from nothing, and be somebody and make your mark in history.

THOMAS COX

> Tupac's late uncle Thomas Cox, or as his friends and family knew him, "T.C.," treated Tupac as if he were one of his own. Most close to Tupac felt that the strong work ethic he had throughout his life was inspired by T.C.

In our house, it didn't matter who the kids belonged to, no one got more than the other. That's how we've always raised our kids. That's how Tupac was raised.

When he was poor, Pac saw that the people who *had* weren't giving it to the people who *didn't* have. He just never understood that. Even as a young kid, Tupac wanted to do something to help. He believed that everyone deserved the same chances in life.

Tupac decided at a very young age that one of the things he was going to do was give back to the community. He wanted to open a youth center so that kids would have a place to go to get off the streets, a place where they would learn skills and have job training. For the kids who he couldn't help at the center, he wanted to reach them with a newsletter that he wanted to put together. He wanted to help anybody who needed it.

For me, even after he became famous, Tupac never changed. He was always very committed to his family, always just a nice person in general, unless you made him angry. Then that was a different story. If you did Tupac wrong, or even just something unjust, he was gonna get you back. I remember once when I was in California with him and we were going to the Soul Train Music Awards. We saw this guy slapping this woman out in the street. Tupac jumped out of the car, chased the guy down the street, and beat him up. If Tupac saw a weaker person being taken advantage of by a stronger person, he just couldn't let it go.

Yeah, he was a movie star and a rapper, but mainly he was a leader.

At the video shoot for "All Bout You."

DONALD HICKEN

> Tupac earned acceptance into the prestigious Baltimore School for the Arts, and was enrolled in a drama course taught by Donald Hicken.

When I first met Tupac, I thought he was going to be a handful. He had a smile that had mischief written all over it. His smile was just winning.

One of my earliest memories of him was his name, because it was so unusual. You see lots of unusual names here at Baltimore School for the Arts, but his was really exceptional. During our first class, I called roll, because that's the time that I begin associating names with faces. When I said his name, somebody laughed. Tupac fastened a look on that person, and the message was clear: *You don't laugh at my name . . . you laugh at my name, and you're in big trouble.* In fact, I think he even said something to that effect. And he was serious. It was never an issue again. And that was the first time I realized we were dealing with a very powerful soul.

He had a wonderful sense of irony, a great sense of humor. So much so that he got himself into trouble here the first semester. He was used to being funny, used to making fun of everything. He ended up on probation because he didn't take the academic part of school seriously. It wasn't so much that he was a poor student. He was very bright and he had the capability, but he didn't have the study skills. He was a cut-up in class. He didn't pay attention. He would just fool around and make jokes and distract the other students. He continually engaged in the process of disrupting the class. I think he had come to the school accustomed to establishing himself socially by being the class clown. He was incredibly fast on his feet, very fast, and very, very witty. But I think he learned within a few months that there's no such thing as a class clown here. This is School for the Arts, and everybody in the theater department here used to be class clown.

When you're in an environment where everybody's talented, I think it's natural to start to look around and go, "Whoa. I need to establish myself through my work as an artist, because being class clown may not be enough." I think Tupac realized this, and he learned that it wasn't enough just to crack people up in algebra class. That may do it at Dunbar, the school where he was before here, but it wasn't going to work at School for the Arts.

Tupac was a young man who seemed to delight in and savor every aspect of being alive. He was just alive in every moment. That's the kernel of creativity . . . being able to be completely perceptive about what's going on. Having a deep perception of life, moment-to-moment, is really what it takes to be an artist, and Tupac clearly had that. He was also just tremendously fun to be around. The girls went nuts for him. He made out like a bandit. By the time he left here, he was dating the most beautiful girls in the school.

When Tupac was in my class, we did an exercise to warm up to each other. I asked the students to create a little movement piece, or a little theater scene. The soundtrack should be their favorite song, or a song that spoke to them. I knew Tupac had been writing raps, because I'd hear him in homeroom. He'd sit there with Jada [Pinkett Smith] and some other people in a circle, and they would read raps to each other that they had written the night before. It was a lively atmosphere. Rap was relatively new then, so their group was hip and kind of exciting. But I didn't know what Tupac was going to bring in for this soundtrack exercise, because there wasn't a lot of rap music available at the time.

Tupac brought in the Don McLean song "Vincent (Starry Starry Night)," which is about how misunderstood the artist Van Gogh was. Tupac had this thing about Van Gogh. He talked about him a lot, he really related to him as an artist, because Van Gogh was a man who was not appreciated in his own time. Van Gogh was a very misunderstood person. Why exactly he related to Vincent Van Gogh, I don't know, but he really did. He loved his work and he loved that song. Tupac did a beautiful movement piece to it, a short story told through movement. It was kind of like a dance where he walked around the room looking for something lost. It was very simple.

I don't think Tupac had been around white people that much before he came to this school. I think he had a fairly implanted chip on his shoulder about white people. And I think that what he learned here was that when you take away the power structure element of white culture, and you get down to the grassroots level of white culture, it's very easy to relate across the races. Tupac's best friend while he was here was a preppy white guy from Gilford, the richest neighborhood in Baltimore. His name was John Cole, and he was a visual artist. John gave Tupac clothes. I have a picture of *Tupac* in a crewneck sweater, standing with his ensemble. You say to yourself, "My God, Tupac in a crewneck sweater!?" But that's because it was John Cole's—they were great friends.

Tupac came back and visited me after he became a recording star, so I got to know him sort of post-fame. I saw fame was affecting his life. I tried very hard to be an influence but I couldn't. I didn't see him often enough. But I think he came to visit because he respected me and wanted my approval. The influences in his post-fame life were just so powerful. The last time I saw him was in my office, and when he was getting up to leave I grabbed a hold of him and said, "You know, you're in this business, this crazy business where the more dangerous you are, the more CDs you sell." I told him, "You are going to sell more CDs dead than alive. And that is the business you're in." I had been saying to him, "You're an actor. You've got to be an actor. And you've got to separate your life from your work in that way. I mean, you meet Arnold Schwarzenegger and you don't expect him to throw you through a plate glass window." I told him that when someone meets Tupac Shakur, they didn't have to meet this thug. That's the Tupac that we see in a video or when we hear one of his raps. But that didn't have to be him. He didn't have to *live* that life. I told him he had to separate that or it was going to eat him up. I told him to think of it as acting, and try to get back into his acting. And I used to tell him to try to get some diverse roles for Chrissake . . . or they would put him in a box because that's the way Hollywood works.

There's a scene in *Gridlock'd* where Tupac's character and his co-star are in an unemployment office. It's a fabulous scene. You can see what wonderful comic timing Tupac had, what a great sense of performance he had, and such a real flair for character. I think he liked the journey to character. And I think in many ways what attracted him to this sort of gangster persona was that it *was* a character. The only tricky part was that he had to live it always, he couldn't just be it at times. The mentality in the rap music world is that you can't be phony.

When we would talk in my office, I tried to get him to understand the issue of authenticity. For me, it was all about authenticity of performance, not authenticity of life. An artist is an artist because of that separation. There's a journey, there's a transformation that takes place. All art is transformation of nature. And if you take away that transformation, you just start living this and doing this. If you diminish it as art, it's just you. But I think Tupac had a completely different take on it. He was not going to be a phony. He needed to be authentic. He needed to be real. What he wrote was what he lived.

STARRY NIGHT

Dedicated in memory of
Vincent Van Gough

a creative heart, obsessed with satisfying
This dormant and uncaring Society
u have given them the stars at night
and u have given them Bountiful Bouquets of Sunflowers
But 4 u There is only contempt
and though u pour your into that frame
and present it so proudly
this world could not accept your Masterpieces
from the heart

So on that starry Night
u gave 2 us and
u took away from us
The one thing we never acknowledged
your Life

Tupac's tribute to Vincent Van Gogh, written when he was nineteen.

JADA PINKETT SMITH

> Tupac and Jada's friendship was born in Baltimore and grew from their love of acting and similar family backgrounds. It lasted the rest of Tupac's life, through their teen years, his incarceration, and their growing fame. Tupac once said of her, "Jada's my heart. She will be my friend my whole life. We'll be old together. Jada can ask me to do anything and she can have it. She can have my heart, my liver, my lungs, my kidney, my blood marrow, all of that."

Tupac and I met at Baltimore School for the Arts. It was the first day, and we had a big seminar where all the theatrical classes were gathering. He came over to introduce himself. In high school, Pac was a little funny-looking, very charismatic. He wasn't necessarily the type of cat I would deal with. But as soon as he approached me, he had this magnificent smile and this great laugh. He was like a magnet. Once you paid attention to him, he kind of sucked you in. We hit it off. We had a connection. Once we got to know each other, we realized what the connection was all about. We were lifelong friends.

Baltimore, through the eyes of myself and Tupac, was drug-infested, rundown, and dark. That was the Baltimore we were from. Of course Baltimore has many different subcultures, which Pac and I had the opportunity to experience through attending the School for the Arts, but the actual neighborhoods we were from were not the best. It was a great escape for both of us, and probably saved both our lives.

Pac was always intense, extremely passionate. He loved Shakespeare. He was very raw. In actors' terms, he was very rough around the edges. You could tell he was new at it, but it was something that was a part of him. Acting was a part of his spirit. He really loved it.

Pac would tell me all the time, "Jada, you're gonna be a star." He'd say, "You got it, you just got it." We talked of big dreams. Pac always wanted to be a rap artist. At that time Rakim was his idol. We always talked about making it. We were just gonna make it—whatever that was. I don't think either of us ever thought we would make it in the way that we did, but we knew we were gonna do something.

Tupac and Jada, mid-1990s.

Pac was definitely an activist. He put the information in the music. He had the mentality that we as young black people needed to be a community. He was very motivating, very pro-active. Pac was the first one who really explained the Black Panther Party to me. My family taught me about the whole Martin Luther King movement, and the Civil Rights Movement, but when Pac came into the picture, he schooled me about Malcolm X and the Black Panther Party. He didn't just talk it—he lived it. He was a seeker of truth.

He was one of my best friends. He was like a brother. It was beyond friendship for us. It's really difficult to explain, because the type of relationship we had, you only get once in a lifetime. He was like a brother and a father figure to me. He was very protective. We took really good care of each other—the best that we could. We gave each other a lot.

We were able to act together one time. I told him that I wanted him to come on *A Different World*. He was so authentic and so real. He was raw energy and pure talent. We had a lot of fun on that show. He played my ex-boyfriend Piccolo from Baltimore, trying to get me back from Bumper, who was playing my boyfriend on the show. It was so Pac because Pac was always like that with me. He'd always be like, "You're seeing who? Whatever, that cat can just beat it." Even though he and I could never be together, he didn't think anyone was good enough for me. Nobody! So when they wanted to write that role, I was like, "This is how it should flow." And it just fit right into the dynamics of our relationship, and it was nothing foreign to either one of us. He just walked right in and just blew up the spot.

He never really got a chance to see me and Will [Smith] together. But the last time I saw Pac, we had a huge argument about it. I don't think that he disapproved of Will. I think it was just that he wasn't happy that I had found *that* guy. Out of all the boyfriends I ever had, Pac still remained the first cat. When Pac called, I jumped. I don't care who I was laid up with. And I think he knew that was gonna change when I met Will. But it wasn't that he disapproved of Will as a person. I think he feared the change in the dynamic of our relationship.

I don't know if Pac ever felt that he could have the crossover acceptance that Will has. There's really no comparison with the two. They're so extremely different, yet so much alike in many different ways. But as far as their philosophies on life in general, those were a little different. The foundation of who Will is explains why he can do the things that he does. I think Pac would have been as loved and respected and as popular as Will, but for much different reasons. Pac could've had it all. He could've had whatever he wanted. He chose a different route.

Tupac had a genuine love for people. He had a genuine love and understanding of what the majority of people were going through, and he had a talent for being able to communicate in such a passionate, wholehearted, all-feeling way. When you heard Pac's voice, there was something about it that would just grab you. There was something about when you'd see him on TV talking. His eyes, his whole being, would just absorb you. He just had a true love for what people were going through. He took on the world.

I think people connected to that passion. They connected to that heart, to that soul. He was so in touch. As strong as he was, he wasn't afraid to show how vulnerable he was. It was a strength; not everybody can do that. It made him so tangible and so human. You felt like you knew him, and he knew you, and he was talking to you in his songs. You'd be thinking, "How does he know me like that?" And I think that's what people miss most about him. It's that connection. Because I don't care how many albums these jokers are selling and how many people want to compare these cats to Tupac—there is nobody, *nobody* like that man. I don't care how many records you sell. I don't care how popular you are. And it pisses me off when people try to compare him. There is no comparison. None. *None*. And I don't know when there ever will be.

I remember when he wrote "Dear Mama." He called me and said, "I wrote this song about our mothers and I want you to hear it." I was like, wow. Both of us had mamas who were addicts. That was one of the things that, when we were younger, we really connected over. 'Cause we were struggling for just basic survival. Where you gonna get your food? Where you gonna get your clothes? What shoes you gonna put on your feet? How you gonna keep the lights on in the house?

When I heard "Dear Mama," it gave me a rush of emotions—it still does when I hear it. I marvel at his ability to be in a situation where he could reveal that about his mother. He could share the pain and the loss and the love and the undeniable connection that you have to your mother, no matter what's going on. It's what we children of addicts all feel and struggle with, and it manifests itself in different ways. I was like, "Damn, how does your mom feel about that?" He was basically like, "It is what it is." I always admired him for that. That was a strength he had that I did not at that particular time in my life. It's not until recently that I've been able to reveal that my mother was also an addict. I would never have said that at the time he did. I would never have revealed that to anybody.

I went to see Pac when he was in prison, in Rikers, which had to be one of the most humiliating experiences I had ever had. I could imagine what he felt like, being behind bars. I felt scared and helpless. We were in this glass circular room with people just watching us.

We couldn't have any privacy. I wanted to hold him and hug him and Lord knows I had been to enough jails to visit other jokers—let's not get that twisted—but for some reason, I thought it would've been different. It was a complete reality check for me. He was in jail. And all that Tupac-ism shit didn't work in here. Then I went to see him when they took him upstate to Dannemora. I went to see him twice, I believe. He needed that. He was like, "Please come see me." We wrote each other back and forth constantly.

Jail changed him big time. He was not the same when he got out. He was a completely different person to me. The Pac that I knew was inside of him still, but he wasn't as hopeful. He wasn't as spirited. He was very angry. He felt betrayed, and on many different levels. And he felt like, "Fuck it. Ain't nobody here for me." I think going to jail made him really realize who loved him and who didn't, and who was down for him, and who wasn't. All the cats that he was writing the music for, he just got a real reality check and I think it was too much for him to bear. I think he got a real dose of what was really going on. I think he was like, fuck it, I'm all for self now. And that just splintered him, because that is not who Pac was. That is not his personality. That is not spiritually how he gets down. He very much believed and tried his best to live the African concept of "I am you and you are me—and I can't be without the we and the we can't be without the me without the you." That all changed.

Pac died without us speaking. The last time I saw him was at this Jamaican restaurant across the street from the Hotel Nikko. We had it out like all the other major times. I can laugh about it now. People ask me if I have regrets, but I'm like, no, because that's just how we were. We were constantly not speaking to each other. It just so happened that he was murdered before we had a chance to reconcile. But I know that when he left that restaurant, he knew that I loved him, and I know that he loved me. So I don't have any pain or regret about not speaking to him before he died.

I was in New York City celebrating my birthday and working on the movie *Woo* when I heard he was shot. I remember calling Afeni and saying, "Fe, do I need to get on a plane right now?" She said, "Jada, he's gonna be okay. You get here when you can." Will had come in to celebrate my birthday, and then I was going to fly to Vegas to see Tupac. I remember that day, September 13, we had just come back from seeing the musical *Rent*. We didn't stay for the whole play. I was ready to go.

We were in the hotel room. I had my whole family there: my mother, Will's mother, Will's grandmother. Sheree—Will's ex-wife—called him. Will looked at me, and said, "Sheree, let me call you back." He said, "Jada, Sheree just said that Pac is dead." I said, "She don't know what the fuck she's talking about. How the fuck she . . . she don't know nothing." I was ready to call Sheree back and lay her out. Lay her out! Just then, my mother, who had gone back to her room, knocked on our door. Will opened it. As soon as I saw her face, I knew he was gone.

My legs just buckled and I dropped to my knees. But the weird thing was, I felt this relief. This load just lifted off and then I fell. And I think that was me knowing that he was okay, but me selfishly not wanting to let go yet.

I was mad at Afeni for a long time because I felt like if he was gonna die, I should've been there. But now that I'm a mother, I understand why Fe said that—you don't think that your child is gonna go. And I'm really happy that I didn't see him like that. I'd much rather have the last sight of him cussing me out in that restaurant, strong, alive, vibrant, than me having to see him laid up in that hospital, because if that had been the last image . . . . I'm just happy that I remember him the way that I do. And I know for a fact that he wouldn't have wanted me to see him like that.

Tupac's story is so complicated. It will never be told completely without him here. You have to understand, five people lived in that cat. You had the political activist. The young man that loved to go out and party, get drunk and get high, which oftentimes would bring a cloud of confusion. And he wasn't always clear, because he was often in an altered state. You had the artist, the fighter, the lover. I mean, come on, there were ten Tupacs in one. He was just a really layered individual. There was nothing simple about him.

> In 2007, the Will and Jada Smith Foundation donated one million dollars to the Baltimore School for the Arts to help pay for a new state-of-the-art theater. She dedicated the donation to Tupac.

JOHN COLE

> John and Tupac's friendship, which began at the Baltimore School for the Arts, challenged stereotypes. The fact that Tupac, a theater major, was from one of the worst parts of Baltimore, and John, a visual artist, was from one of the wealthiest didn't affect their connection.

Tupac lived in an area known for being a drug hotspot. There were a lot of drug dealers around, so he hung out some with them. But he wasn't selling drugs—he was going to the School for the Arts and trying to be more artistic, more centered in the arts than centered on being a thug. But that's what he went home to at night. Even in his neighborhood he was an outsider—people in that area wouldn't accept you unless you'd lived there for a long time, so he really didn't hang out there that much. When we met, he started hanging out at some of the parties I went to. We used to drive around in my brother's VW a lot, not really doing much, just driving around and trying to get into something. Jada's cousin, Jada, Tupac, and I hung out all the time. We were a close-knit group.

My life and Tupac's life had some parallels; both of us grew up without a father, and both of us had mother figures as our role models. Because of this, we both had a lack of understanding of the male world to a degree. When you grow up like we did, you don't really get how it's supposed to be. We weren't raised to be the jock with the male macho bravado, "look who I can beat up" or "look who I can mac on." We were pretty close in a lot of ways, and I believe this is one of the reasons.

I miss Tupac's laugh, and what a pain in the ass he could be. I miss how he could make light of certain situations, and bring another perception. Few people can do that.

Tupac was definitely into getting attention. I like to be entertained. Just one more reason why we got along so well. He was always on stage. He was always entertaining, always hammin' it up. We'd go to parties and he'd be doing stand-up, with ten or fifteen people around him cracking up. He would do different characters. One of my favorites was this old drunk black man named Redbone who was always staggering around running into things. Redbone would always get on my nerves after a while. Tupac would stay in character for two or three days at a time. I'd say, "Look, you gotta do something else. I'm really getting sick of Redbone."

John playing with Tupac's niece and nephew, Nzingha and Malik.

After Tupac moved to California, we didn't interact again until he invited me out there to hang out while he was a dancer with Humpty. Then when he was shooting *Poetic Justice* he asked me to come out again. When he got into all the thug stuff, that really wasn't so interesting to me. That was so predictable. It's not the most creative thing. I think he eventually got bored of that role, but he was stuck. Maybe the only way to get out of that role was to die.

NOTHING CAN COME BETWEEN US
4 JOHN

let's NOT talk of MONey
let us forget The WORLD
4 a moment let's Just revel
in our eternal comradery
in my Heart I KNOW
there will NEVER BE a DAY
that I DoN't remember
the times we shared
u were a friend
when I was at my lowest
and being a friend 2 me
was NOT easy NoR fashionable
Regardless of how popular
I become u remain
My unconditional friend
unconditional in it's truest Sense
Did u think I would forget
Did u 4 one moment Dream
that I would ignore u
if so Remember this from here 2 forever
Nothing Can Come between us

A poem Tupac wrote in his teens about John.

CHAKA

> Tupac and Chaka started out together as Panther children, and although their journeys through life took different courses, they both ended up in the music industry. Chaka worked his way up from an intern at Jive Records to the CEO of a record label he co-owns with Ludacris.

When we were young, there were times Tupac and I were around each other constantly. There were times we lived together in the Bronx. And then there were times we wouldn't see each other for months. Our parents were brothers and sisters in the struggle. Throughout Pac's life and throughout all of our lives, we were outcasts because of the way we were raised. We wanted to be like the normal kids, but we had African names, and we dressed differently, and we were taught differently. The excitement Pac and I used to have when we saw each other was because we recognized that we were so alike. We would have so much fun together. One of the places we used to meet was called BANA, basically a hospital where holistic medicine was practiced. It was also a place where all the revolutionaries, all of our parents and aunts and uncles, would get together. It was a four-story brownstone and it was huge. We would run wild, from the basement to three or four stories up.

Pac was fun-loving and calm, but in certain situations he would always defend what he felt. I remember one time we were running around playing hide and seek in this one office with this old desk and leather chair. His sister, Set, was playing with us. Something happened and I ended up pushing her and she bumped her head. If you look at her head, she still has the scar. She cried so hard. Of course I'm saying, "I'm sorry, I didn't mean it." And I was scared. Pac got so mad, we had a fight. I guess he felt like I did it on purpose. It was just his nature to be protective of those he cared about or loved.

We saw each other off and on up until '88 when he popped up in Atlanta. He came to Morehouse to see me. There was a celebration on campus and he performed. He rapped a few songs, hard-hitting political songs that blew everybody away. Afterward, we ran around campus acting silly. He told me, "You leave this college thing alone. Come on the road with us." This was when he was about to pop off with Digital Underground. I wasn't about to run up and leave, but I wanted to. My mother and family wouldn't have been supportive.

He came back again to visit when he was on a big tour with Heavy D, Shock G and Digital, Luke, and all them. I went to the hotel to see him. Tupac took me down to the lobby, and Shock was down there at the piano. Girls were in the lobby, and I was like, "Is this what life is like?" I ended up challenging Flavor Flav to a Flavor Flav dance. It was pure buffoonery.

Then "Same Song" came out, and he was on with Digital. Then the movie *Juice* came out. We were watching him going and going, but he was still just Tupac. He hadn't created Thug Life yet. He didn't have an entourage or anything yet. What was funny was that when he came out with "Same Song," his stepbrother Mopreme came out with his own record. And I'd watch his video on TV and I'd be like, "That's Mo." Then I'd see the "Same Song" video and I'd say, "That's my cousin, too."

Pac came back to visit later after he started Thug Life, and we went to this Malcolm X Grassroots dinner at Pascal's hotel. He gave this amazing speech that night. He cut loose. I was like, "Whoa." I started seeing some of his anger coming out, and flashes of who he was going to become.

I was an intern at Jive Records when I first started in the industry. When Tupac was in jail, I used to send him all kinds of music I wasn't supposed to be sending anyone. This was when the C.O.s [Correctional Officers] and other staff at the jail were messin' with him so he would never get the stuff I sent to him. They would just hold it. And one time they sent it back. Larry Kahn, the VP of Jive Records, called my boss one day to try to find out who was sending stuff out to Tupac. My boss said, "Do you know Tupac?" I was like, "Uh, yeah." He said, "Are you sending him stuff in jail?" Leave it to Tupac to almost get me fired . . . from in jail.

DAVID SMITH

> The year Tupac attended Tamalpais High School in Marin, he took drama from David Smith.

Tupac was very happy, very calm. He talked to me about wanting to perform Shakespeare and Chekhov. He performed in one of Chekhov's plays, *The Bear*. I remember worrying about whether or not he was going to get his lines together. He was always such a pleasant person, but he never had his stuff together lines-wise. But then he stepped on stage that night and dazzled everybody in the place with that charismatic charm. He was really, really good. He definitely wasn't the perfect study, but he could pull it off when it came time.

Because Tupac is still such a big entity, my students to this day want to soak up all the Tupac stuff they can. When they ask me about him, I always tell them that I knew Tupac for about six months before I even knew he rapped. That wasn't part of his thing in my class at all. He didn't show me any of that side of himself. One day we were sitting in the student center at Tam High, and we were all just hanging out and rehearsing, when one of the students said, "Hey, Tupac, why don't you do that rap for David?"

I looked at him and said, "You rap?" Looking back, that was probably the stupidest thing I've ever said to anybody. I had no idea. Suddenly he busted out with this really, really positive rap about Martin Luther King and all this wonderful, positive stuff. It felt very idealistic and very youthful—the way we all were in the '70s. There was nothing really fancy about it, but it was extraordinarily well-intentioned. That was a great moment for me.

Once I had my guitar on campus, and he asked me if I knew a song called "Vincent (Starry, Starry Night)," by Don McLean. I told him I knew it and he was like, "That's my favorite song!" I told him to sing it with me, but he was quick to say he didn't sing.

I was kind of detached from the whole rap thing. But one day on campus I ran into Tupac during a time he was no longer at Tam and he said, "Hey, David, I'm in Digital Underground!" I didn't know who they were, so I said, "Oh, is that a good thing?" So he had to explain to me who they were. Then I heard he was in a few movies. And soon after that, I was walking through the record store and I saw *2pacalypse Now*. The lyrics were something like, "Fuck the Police. Fuck the Sheriff's Department. Fuck the this. Fuck the that." I thought to myself, "Wow, he's really a long way from that idealistic, Martin Luther King stuff."

DARRELL ROARY

> Darrell Roary met Tupac in Marin City, California, when Tupac moved from Baltimore to the West Coast.

I met Tupac the summer that I came back to Marin from college up in Washington. He had come to Tam High a year after I graduated. I remember my first thoughts were, "Who is this guy with the weird clothes and the gold Gumby hair?" He had paint on his jeans, and "Free Mandela" written on his clothes.

Soon after he moved into Marin City, he became this "neighborhood" child. A lot of people took him in. In Marin City, you were either involved in sports or just living the normal teenage life. He came in and added a twist to everything with his talent, the polka dots, and his gold hair.

He was doing the music thing at that time. He used to carry this notepad around with him, everywhere we went. Everywhere. You know how a kid carries around a favorite blanket or a football? That's how he was. We'd be leaving the house and we'd say "Tupac, come on, leave the book at home." He used to write in it all the time. And people ask today where is all his music coming from? Well, imagine that he was writing all the time way back then when I knew him. I mean, that was when he was only, like, seventeen years old. Tupac had so much knowledge oozing out of him that he just had to put it on paper. He wrote for the love of writing.

Today it's just a trip how worshipped Tupac is. When I go visit my relatives in South Carolina, all my cousin's friends come over to the house and sit down and ask me all these questions about him, and ask me to tell stories about him. It's crazy to hear his name in sitcoms and movies. There's always going to be a Tupac reference, for the rest of our lives. It's almost like he's become the quintessential symbol of rap music.

Darrell and Tupac.

WHO'S THIS GUY TWO-PACK?

"I feel proud that I helped him get his start. He had enormous talent and unfortunately I feel his best work was still ahead of him. The saddest part about this is that no one will ever know what he might have become."

—Ernest Dickerson

RAY LUV

> Ray Luv was one of Tupac's closest friends during the time he lived in the Bay Area. They started a group called Strictly Dope together just months before Tupac signed with Interscope Records.

"Trapped" was actually a song that I wrote, but I just didn't feel the vibe. I crumpled it up and threw it away. Just part of it was stickin' out of the garbage can and this nigga came in, and we were sitting there hella high. Tupac pulled the paper out of the garbage, started reading it, and he said, "Ah, this is dope. What the fuck you throw this away for?" I told him I didn't want it. He asked if he could have it. He read it and was like, "Man, this shit is dope." So I gave it to him. It was purely on love. I wasn't looking for no bread.

Later he called me up and told me he had just recorded it as a single. He said "We want it to be the first fuckin' single." And then he told me he was gonna shoot me a couple G's, which he did, and we was even. When that shit came on MTV, I was sitting next to him. We were eating and waiting for the video to come on. We kept saying, "Man, it's gonna be on today, I know it's gonna be on today, I think it's gonna be on today." We just sat there waiting and eating original Buffalo wings. Dr. Dre and Ed Lover premiered the video and we went crazy. We drove to Marin City after that and got fucked up all night long. Then when "Trapped" went to number one on MTV, I was just speechless. I couldn't believe it. I wrote that shit. I thought, "Damn, we really doin' something."

Writing poetry is how we initially got close. That's how we got to know one another so well—through our poetry and our music, through our stories, our troubles. There was so much to say. I lost my mama when I was young. He never knew his father.

One year Pac had Christmas dinner over at my dad's house. My father is a southern man. He believes in hard work. He believes in education. He believes if you have a good education and you got a will to bust your ass, you can have the whole world. So we're at dinner and he asks me and Pac, "What's up with school with you brothas?" And we said, "Man, we got this rap shit, you know what I'm sayin'?" At the time Pac had already signed, so that was good enough for us. Back then, we didn't realize that signing ain't shit.

I can out-talk nine out of ten people, but the two people in life that I could never out-talk were Pac and my father. So you can imagine what kind of conversation this was. It was

Ray and Tupac at a Mac Mall video shoot.

like an argument without yelling. It went on . . . and on . . . and on. Pac told my dad, "I feel that you get your education in the world. You get your education in the streets, by being around people, by learning who the fake ones are, who the real ones are, who you want to emulate, who you don't want to be like." So my father responded with, "What's the use of being hard and having a revolution if all the revolutionaries are locked up or dead? Then all you are is a memory. We got a whole bunch of them."

Then my dad said, "Y'all brothers are smart, you're intelligent, you need to get back in school." And Pac's attitude was straight up, fuck that shit.

Pac went further than everybody else. He was willing to do more than everybody else. Pac did not sleep. You know how niggas say, "I don't sleep." That nigga did not fuckin' sleep. No drugs. No nothing. And with the way we was smoking weed, that's a fuckin' amazing thing. We would stay up 'til four o'clock in the morning, and then had to be on location at seven a.m. Niggas showin' up, hella tired, Pac would be out there dressed, fit, energized, smoking a blunt, telling muthafuckas what to do.

For someone so articulate, so fuckin' intelligent, the muthafucka could fuck up some food. When he'd eat hamburgers, he'd just have hella shit all over his face and all over everything. And the way he cooked, he just tore *up* the kitchen every time. He was so messy. He was an incredible cook, though—he could make Top Ramen taste like gumbo. He'd put a lot of garlic in it, a lot of onions, some seasoning. That's some broke shit, to be able to do that. You can tell when a muthafucka has been broke for awhile.

I never saw no retreat, no fear from the dude, never. Not even fear of death. I think his only fear was not being accepted. If there was any fear, it was of that.

ATRON GREGORY

> Tupac's first manager, Leila Steinberg, introduced him to Atron Gregory, the president
of TNT Records, in the late 1980s. Atron became his manager and began searching for a
recording contract.

After Leila Steinberg introduced me to Tupac and Ray Luv, she and I had a conversation.
One of us was going to work with Ray, and one of us was going to work with Tupac. She was
happy with either because she felt that they both had the same amount of talent. My choice
was to take Tupac. She would continue working with Ray, and we would work together as it
made sense.

I took Tupac to Shock G to get his opinion, and soon after, began getting his demo out.
During this time, Tupac was given the opportunity to become the president of the New
Afrikan Panthers. If he became the leader of that group, he would have had to leave California and assume the responsibility, but he wanted to do music and to act. He had this love for
both politics and entertainment. He wanted to do his political work through the medium of
entertainment. And he wanted his record deal now. He was tired of waiting. He was very
frustrated during this time. Tupac was not one to wait for anybody. I told Shock we had to
do something or else we'd lose him. That's when Shock decided to take him out on tour.

There were so many tour stories, but one that stuck with me the most was from when
we were in Oklahoma City. The hotel was a block and a half away from the convention center where we were performing. Someone had either gone poking in Tupac's dressing room,
or busted in and stole something from Public Enemy—I can't remember exactly. Tupac was
determined to find out who did it. He kept saying, "I'll find out. I know who did it." The
point wasn't that whatever had been stolen had a lot of value; it was more of a principle
thing. We were like a big family, as opposed to different crews fighting against each other.

A few of us were sitting in the hotel lobby, when all of a sudden this guy comes running through the door, and here come Tupac chasing him and yelling. Tupac had found out
he was the thief. The guy dives over the counter of the reception desk to get away. Everyone
else runs over and grabs Tupac, and the guy jumps back over the counter and runs out the
door. It was just the funniest thing to see—first this guy running through the door, and then
Tupac following and screaming and hollering, "That's him! That's him!" It was just one of

those things you'll never forget. What's funny is that no one really cared in the first place. The guy got out the door and no one ever saw him again.

A lot of labels passed on Tupac. Sylvia Rhone passed. Tommy Boy passed. Laura Hines, the woman who did press for Tommy Boy, tried to convince Monica Lynch to sign Tupac, but she couldn't. Laura was one of the few people who kept saying that she knew he was going to be a star. Another person was Jeff Fenster. Jeff Fenster, at Charisma Records, was really the only one at first who wanted to sign Tupac, but the company wouldn't let him. They were primarily doing a lot of rock and roll.

After I sent the demo to Tom Whalley at Interscope Records, he called to say he wanted to meet Tupac. Tupac came down to L.A. to meet him. I think it was probably Tupac's first real business meeting. It ended up being a very simple dinner, and we didn't necessarily talk about anything particular, it was just chitchat. It was a get-to-know-you type of dinner, where they wanted to find out about me, and about Tupac. I've gone to several business dinners over the years, and some of them can be very obtrusive. Labels want to know every little thing about your life, down to who your grandparents are. Everything. It wasn't that type of dinner.

Two days later, they called. They wanted to give Tupac a deal.

TOM WHALLEY

> Tom Whalley, the chairman and CEO of Warner Bros. Records, was a partner at Interscope Records when he met Tupac. Immediately, he recognized Tupac's potential and offered him his very first recording contract.

I became interested in Tupac after hearing his demo in 1990. He was one of the first artists I approached to sign to Interscope. He was in L.A., flying out of the Burbank airport to go to the Bay Area, so I drove to meet him in a Holiday Inn restaurant.

I was blown away by how articulate and direct Tupac was—he knew who he wanted to be as an artist. Also, he was incredibly personable and had a great sense of humor. He just had an aura. I left that first meeting with him incredibly excited. I knew he had something important to say and that he would create meaning with his art. He must have felt it too, because he signed with Interscope.

Tupac recorded a tremendous amount of music. He would write five to ten songs a day depending on his mood, but a lot of the songs he left behind are incomplete, which was very typical of him. He would hear a beat he liked, throw some rhymes on top of it, then move on to the next one, so there's a lot of unfinished material that needs additional production. I think it's really important that his fans have the chance to hear everything he had to say. All his music needs to be heard, which is why I stayed involved after his death. I understood him, and to this day I remain true to his spirit.

It was amazing to watch Tupac's creative process in the studio, but it had its challenges and we had our disagreements. He didn't have a lot of patience and he moved a thousand miles a minute. If I made a suggestion, his first response was always "no." Every time. But if he'd said "yes" to all my suggestions, he wouldn't have been a great artist. More often than not, Tupac would digest what I'd suggested, then improve on it, and in the end he'd be happy with the result. We had a relationship based on trust—he knew that I'd be straight with him.

To understand Tupac, you really have to know his mother, and when you get to know Afeni, you realize that they were almost twins. He was just like her in how he saw and reacted to the world. Afeni became politicized at a young age, as a member of the Black Panthers. Her history is the connection to the politics in his music. Music became a way for him to express the wrongs he perceived in life. They were of different generations, but they shared a need to express themselves that came out in very similar ways.

I'm probably an unlikely friend for them to have, because we are so different, but we just had a connection. They trusted me and I trusted them. After Tupac passed, Afeni had to cope with losing her son and all that that involved, past, present and future. She needed to know there was someone to turn to whom she could confide in, and she found that someone in me.

Afeni and Tom Whalley.

LORI EARL

> Though Lori Earl was a veteran publicist when she met Tupac, her work translating the young, complicated artist to the media was one of the toughest challenges of her career. Nevertheless, she says the time she worked with Tupac made up some of her best and most memorable years.

I remember Tom [Whalley] telling me that we signed a guy named Tupac. Back then, we didn't even know how to pronounce his name. Half the people would see his name and call him "Two-pack." In fact, his original bio reads, "Two-pock" so people would know how to say it.

From the very first day I started working with him, it was just crazy. I didn't go to his first photo shoot, but I remember the photographer calling me, hysterical because Tupac had shown up with a bunch of guys with guns. Despite the circumstances, the photographer didn't give up, and he still managed to get the shot.

So much of what I did was to try to explain Pac to the media. He was always a target, election years in particular. Rap lyrics would always become a campaign issue and Tupac was at the top of their list.

It was so frustrating. People were always trying to make his lyrics negative by taking them out of context. I was constantly trying to get people to look at his songs in their entirety. No matter what I did, the media would ultimately state the opposite of what Tupac's message actually was; they never took the time to look at what Tupac was really saying. It was always poetry. He'd be rapping it, but it was still poetry, no different than what Bob Dylan and Marvin Gaye did for their generations.

There were always injustices. He was charged with shooting at two cops in Atlanta, but it turns out they were off duty, drunk, and had not identified themselves as police. The media made such a big deal of the case when it initially happened, but then they never went back and explained the outcome. It was never interesting enough for them to report Tupac's innocence. If you ever followed anything that was happening to him through to the end, you would realize that his actions were always for a reason. If there was violence involved, it was never frivolous. He was never a violent guy but he was fearless when it came to standing up for what he believed in.

One of my biggest frustrations when I worked with Tupac was when he was charged with sexual abuse, a misdemeanor. Even the *New York Times* got it wrong and called it a sexual assault (which is a felony). Then of course it would perpetuate as different outlets would pick up and continue the inaccuracy. The media didn't take the time to make the corrections, even after my calls.

DEAREST Ms. Lori Earle,

In Life We Rarely Appreciate the finer things. We hardly stop to Notice the most wonderful things. We constantly take for granted what we believe will always be there. I have. But I have also taken Notice of what I have so many times ignored. Please accept my apologies 4 not showing you how truly overjoyed I am 2 have U as part of my team. Please Accept my Thanx and gratitude as a Small token of appreciation. Continue 2 keep the faith

With Much Love,
Tupac

This letter, which Tupac sent to Lori from prison in 1995, is one of her most prized possessions.

I was always frustrated by the lack of press recognition he received. Looking back, it's insane to think about how hard we had to work to get him a write-up. Today, that sounds like it would be easy, like, "Well, of course you would." But while he was alive, nobody got it. He didn't get a *Rolling Stone* cover until he died. There was a time we couldn't even get a TV crew to cover a video shoot for one of the songs off *2Pacalypse Now*. It was hard to get people to pay attention to the art, because there was always so much other drama there to distract them. What made it worse was knowing that he was so extraordinary. No one had ever done what he did. The video for "Brenda's Got a Baby" still makes me cry. And there's "Dear Mama." Now that I have two sons of my own, I think I appreciate that song more than when it was released. It's so unfortunate that songs like those got lost in all the chaos.

Of course this is Tupac, so sometimes he didn't help matters. After one of the trials, he came out of court and he did that cocky swagger of his and then he spit right at the cameras. Aargh, I died. I knew why he did it, but I knew the media would use it negatively over and over again. I think it's probably some of the most used footage to date.

The second time he was shot, I did not think he was going to die. Nobody did. This was Tupac—he was invincible. I was just waiting for that call confirming that everything was okay. On September 13, I got a call from Death Row's publicist, George Pryce. I can still hear George say the words, "He's gone." The night he died, I sat in my room alone and cried. I didn't know what to do with my grief. So I wrote a letter to Afeni that was a bunch of scribble. There was no one I could share my sorrow with who would get it.

Working with Tupac was one of the proudest parts of my career. Explaining him to people is part of what I was put here for. Especially people my age, who are finally getting it. But back when I was working with him, my peers would say, "He's just some thug, isn't he?" It would make me so angry. I got into so many fights with people. They didn't get it. I don't have to explain that part of him anymore.

He sent me a letter from jail. It's one of my most prized possessions. I cried so hard when I got it. People just go crazy when I show them. It shows just how far he has come, when people in their fifties and sixties say in disbelief, "You have a letter from Tupac?," whereas before, they acted like, "Who's this guy *Two-pack*?"

There are so many times in my profession when you feel like it's for nothing, it's so frivolous, or your work isn't appreciated. But when I think of the fact that Tupac, somebody I respected so much, wrote this letter to me, it really doesn't matter if anybody else gets it.

SHOCK G

> As frontman for Digital Underground, Shock G gave Tupac a chance to go on his first nationwide tour, introducing him to the world for the very first time. Tupac once said, "Everything I have, I owe to Shock G."

Tupac was first signed to TNT Records with Atron Gregory. Atron asked me to meet him before he signed him, and I did, and I approved. All I knew was that his name was Tupac. He wasn't anybody to me. He was good, but Atron had a lot of good people. He had a whole roster. Atron couldn't get him a deal at first, so he called me and asked, "Can you do something with Tupac? 'Cause I'm about to lose him." I was thinking we didn't need any more rappers, and we only got so many laminates. Some of the dancers and the roadies were interchangeable, so we switched him up with Money B's brother. We told him that if he came, he'd have to carry the same responsibilities that Money's brother was handling. I told him that he'd have to sometimes carry equipment, and learn the Humpty Dance. He said, "Yeah, I'll do it. Anything. That's hot. I'll do anything to get out of here."

On the tour, Pac was immediately hot with the ladies. That's when we really knew he was a star. We were already working on his album and everything, we believed in him, we knew he could rhyme. But we knew he was a star by the way the girls reacted. It was because of Pac that on the first city of the first tour, we had to sneak the bus out of the parking lot. He had this chick on the bus after the show, and her boyfriend and his niggas were around the bus asking, "Yo, is LaToya on there?" We opened the door and we was like, "No, we haven't seen her." But it was funny 'cause the whole time we knew she was on the back of the bus with Pac.

Pac had a thing for Mariah Carey's song "Vision of Love." You always knew Pac was sad if you walked by his room and he was playing it. He had a tape with it playing over and over again.

He had so many different sides to him. Pac was a cut-up, too. Sometimes we'd be picking out our outfits for the show. And he'd grab the Shock G and Humpty wigs and say, "Yo, let me wear this." Sometimes he'd bug out and wear the nose when we were just walking down the street or going to the mall. He had a real kid side to him that suffocated later. I think it was 100 percent still in him, but he just couldn't get to it cause he had so much

Shock G and Tupac flexing.

Shock G, friend Cheeba, and Tupac during Digital's 1990 spring tour.

Shock G and Tupac on tour.

other stuff in his space to deal with. He had to represent the thug side to get cats to hear what he had to say.

On that tour, we actually didn't argue that much. And when we did, it was with a lot of respect for each other, because Pac realized that I was the person who was the center of Digital Underground, and I realized that he was an extremely driven, talented, hot cat. I didn't know he was going to be as big as he became, but I still treated cats with respect if I thought they were gonna even be moderately successful rappers. But we didn't have "Pac" yet. "Pac" was different. I didn't feel the Thug side yet. He was very tough, but he wasn't street tough. He was brave and courageous. But he still didn't have game, and he knew it.

If he were here right now, we'd be arguing. Actually, all our arguments were really just one long argument. He was a hard person to deal with. He couldn't just walk away. The first argument we had wasn't really an argument; I just had to let him know that he couldn't punch the soundman. When we were on tour, we had to try and send Pac home a lot. But he wouldn't go. He would always try to rap over a singer, and he'd say it was because they were losing the crowd. I kept feeling like Frank from *Scarface*, and he was Tony Montana. He would always try to flip the whole show.

We never really thought to put Tupac in Digital officially, because his album was very Public Enemy. Our album was very Whodini or Biz Markie. So we weren't trying to mix Pac up with Digital. But it happened anyway with "Same Song." When we recorded the video, it had a Jamaican, a rock star, a bagpipe player, a Hasidic Jew, and an African king. We were walking around the set and I was explaining what we were gonna do for the video. And I was like, "Music is a common language. We have all these different outfits representing all the same song all around the world, and different nationalities." And I told Money he had to be the Hasidic Jew, and said, "Pac, you gonna be the African king . . . " He was like, "Why I gotta be the African?" But he did it and he did it well; it's funny because he went down in history as an African king. It was beautiful.

When my mother came to the video shoot, she asked, "What's his name, Gregory? That one right there, what's his name? Watch him, he's a star." We knew he was the hottest up-and-coming star in our camp, but at the time we didn't know what he was gonna end up meaning to the world.

During our fifth tour—the "Sons of the P"—after Tupac had left to go do his thing, after he filmed *Poetic Justice*, one morning he surprised us by coming on the tour bus while we were sleeping. I remember hearing his voice. One by one, we started to wake up—everybody just had to hear that nigga. We were proud of that nigga. I think one of the first questions out of someone's mouth was, "Yo, you messing with Janet Jackson?" He came to tell us that he had two weeks off and he wanted to do some shows.

We were sitting on the bus one morning lookin' at *Billboard* magazine, trying to see where our album *Sons of the P* was. It had just reached the top twenty. Tupac started looking for *2Pacalypse Now*—it was in the fifties, and it had risen. I think *Sons of the P* got certified Gold. And *2Pacalypse Now* just broke the 300,000 level. We were trying to convince him, "It's comin,' it's comin'. It's gonna get up there." And he slammed the *Billboard* magazine down and said, "Well, if I could get a beat like 'Kiss You Back' [Digital Underground's current hit] . . . " and walked away. That shit killed me. I was speechless. So I knew I had to take over. I sent him a tape with two beats—"I Get Around" was the first.

I got a message from him. It went like this: "Beeeep . . . Shock, yeah that first beat. I wanna fuck with that. I'm just letting you know. I haven't even listened to the whole thing. I just heard one bar and turned it off to call you. Just had to let you know."

I remember that Pac was trying to get some knowledge about the history of the struggle in America. He learned from Chuck D and he used to fight back from a more political standpoint for a while. Then he started to see the more in-your-face way Ice Cube, Scarface, and Geto Boys were doing it. And then he realized he had more of that in him naturally. He couldn't be Chuck D. He didn't have enough book knowledge, or history, or knowledge of the law to fight racism the way Chuck fought it. But he knew he could fight it like Ice Cube. And that's when he decided to let his nuts hang and go the thug route. And that's when Pac started realizing his strength. He realized that out of the whole Digital camp, he was the one who cats listened to the most. He was the one who lived it the most, the one who had the most absent father, the most food stamps, the most moving around, the most being left to watch TV alone.

I loved Pac like he was my best friend. I loved him like I loved Martin Luther King. Like Malcolm. I loved him like that.

> "I Get Around" was the first single off Tupac's second album, *Strictly 4 My N.I.G.G.A.Z.* In 1993 it climbed the Billboard charts, reaching #5 in Hip Hop charts and #8 in the Rap charts.

YO-YO

> During the time that Tupac was a roadie and dancer for Digital Underground, he met a young pioneering female rapper named Yo-Yo who was just starting out with Ice Cube. Based on their love for rapping, the two became inseparable during the tour.

We used to rap and battle. We used to go out after the shows and walk and talk. He would tell me how he had it hard growing up and how he was homeless. He'd also talk about his father, Mutulu, being in jail. He used to talk about his best friend Jada and how he hadn't seen her in a long time. He was so political and would talk about how he wouldn't turn the other cheek. His rap back then was "Brenda's Got a Baby." He would say it all day long. And he used to have this other rap talking about Malcolm X and Martin Luther King. I always liked him because he was so militant at the time. He was a young soldier and that's what attracted me to him.

I remember he used to smoke, I mean, *chain*-smoke. I asked him why he smoked so much and he'd say he was just stressed out. He was always worried about his career, and his family. He was especially concerned about his sister, Set. He would say, "You gotta make sure Set is going in the right direction." He wanted me to be something like a role model to her.

Our friendship grew because we had so much in common. We were two people just trying to make it. We understood each other's background. I could gripe with him about things that he understood and the same with him. We were both just trying to figure out life at the same time coming from the inner city, the ghetto. And the fact that we were both stars made it so that we could really identify with each other on that level. He really believed in himself all the way. He was cocky. He would always say, "I'm a skinny, big dick, cocky nigga."

We were always hanging out somewhere—one time at his house in North Hollywood, we were all just chillin' and smoking, Stretch and Mike Cooley—even Biggie was there. I remember they were just battling and listening to music. I can still see him with that little white chap stuff on his lips. He used to put so much on that he'd have little white creases on his lips. He'd always have on overalls. He was just so hungry he'd rap anywhere. I would always tell him to write me a song. He was like, "You write me a song, little Yo-Yo." He tried to get me to call him Uncle Pac because he would say he taught me how to rap. He even wrote me a play. He called it, "A Day in the Life of Yo-Yo."

Ultimately Tupac and I became like brother and sister. He'd see me in a club and I'd be wearing a miniskirt and he'd smack me on the butt and say, "Why you got that miniskirt on?" We always had love for each other no matter where we were.

RICHIE RICH

> Fellow rap artist Richie Rich met Tupac early in his career, but never let him forget where he came from.

Pac would often put on a bravado for the friends in his life. But in actuality, he wasn't a real rough guy. He was good in the role of Bishop in *Juice*, but in life he didn't project all that. It wasn't his natural aura. When I say Pac wasn't a tough guy, I don't mean that he was soft, I just mean he wasn't the type of guy you'd be intimidated by. People think that he actually was like Bishop, but if you sat in a room with him, he was just a cool person.

There were times when I think he did kind of become the characters he played. Like in *Poetic Justice*, when he played Lucky's character. Lucky smoked cigarettes. I remember I was on the set and I was like, "What you doin' with that cigarette? I didn't know you smoked." He said, "I don't smoke. Lucky smokes." He was sittin' there studying his lines and pullin' on a cigarette. After the movie was done shooting, there Pac was, smoking cigarettes. I said, "I thought you didn't smoke, I thought that was Lucky." He was like, "Shut up, dude."

When he really started blowin' up, we had this game, "Guess who I fucked?" He would call me and say, "Hey . . . guess who I fucked?" I'd be like, "Who?" He'd say, "Guess." So I would guess all the names of the girls I wanted to fuck, 'cause we had the same taste. And he'd say, "Oh, damn close, I *wish* I could've fucked her, but no, not her." He would just name some of the most surprising people and I knew he would never lie about it. And I'd sit back and say to myself, "This dude is just way out." When I called him and said, "Guess who I fucked?" it never failed that he'd always say, "Already fucked her." But he was joking most of the time.

From the time Tupac got out of prison, it was crackin'. He stayed in the Peninsula hotel in Beverly Hills for months. I can remember coming to that room and Pac having everything—clothes, tennis shoes, everything. Flowers from women. Blunts everywhere. You know the stuff that comes out of the blunt before you fill it? There was a mountain of that stuff, two feet high. People waiting on him hand and foot. He's standing up, getting measured for custom-tailored suits. He's doing photo shoots in the room. He reached in his drawer and it was filled with hundred-dollar bills. He went up to Armani and he bought a belt and two pair of pants and he spent like 3,700 bucks. I was like, "Dude . . . you are trippin'." I mean, at that time I could have filled my closet for $3,700.

E-40

> One of the pioneers of the famous Bay Area lingo and West Coast sound, E-40 was a huge inspiration to Tupac even before they met.

I was introduced to Tupac by Richie Rich. Rich was telling me, "Man, Tupac wants to holler at you. He supports what you're doing and everything. He told me to give you his number." Before that he'd given me and the clique a shout-out on his *Strictly 4 My N.I.G.G.A.Z.* album. I was thinking, "Damn, he recognized *us*?" We were just some little, young, independent cats. We weren't out there like that yet.

We ended up hooking up at the Jack the Rapper conference in Atlanta. We kicked it real tough out there, had big drinks. We was tycoonin'. We was campaignin'. We upheld our bayness . . . me, him, and Treach. When I met him, Tupac was like, "much love, much respect, my nigga. Real niggas need to stick together." But I'm givin' him the same love back. I was like, "You're an innovative man. I'm lovin' everything you doin'. You're a real muthafucka. You speak the real." You know, some real nigga talk, you smell me? So we got down and we kicked it.

We did a song with Tupac when we had our studio on Solano Avenue. I mean, we were right on the main strip, we had a barbershop on one side and a check cashing place on the other side and a Church's Chicken across the street. So everybody knew we were there. And at that time we was funkin' with some niggas from the other side of town so we had to be down there with thumpers and everything. And when we—B-Legit and all of us—write, we like to write on the floor. We take the pen and pad and lay on our bellies and lay on the floor. Tupac comes in with Big Syke and them and they pull up and he's in the Bay so Tupac had his thumper on him. But at the same time it's like we laid on the floor and was fittin' to write. We had the beat going on, had the pow wow, getting perky, doin' the whole little routine that we do and when I got on the floor I had a mini MAC-10 on me so I took it out of my big puff jacket and put it on the woop wop, on the floor right beside me. When I did it like that, it was comedy. We all put our thumpers on the floor and when we did it, Tupac was layin' on the floor right with us, but he had *two* thumpers. He just laid them on the floor and was like, "I'm right here with ya, what's up? I'm withcha." This shit was real life—he had *two* thumpers. We knew we was fitting to get down.

The next day I asked him to come to the video shoot for a song called "Practice Lookin' Hard" on an EP called *The Mail Man*. All the rappers from the Bay were gonna be in it. He told me he had to go to court on the day of the video but he would come through. He and all his dudes showed up and hung out all day. We shot the video at this schoolhouse in the Berkeley-Emeryville area. There were a lot of kids around and he was out there taking pictures with kids and just campaignin'. He was a real good dude, a down-to-earth dude.

Back then we used to smoke these cigarettes called bidis. I was on those things real tough. He was fuckin' with me a little bit about them. But he was showin' everybody how to roll blunts, you smell me? He put down a display of that. Everybody was wearing their Pendleton shirts, those button-down shirts that Eazy-E and them used to wear. They was wearin' those and Dickies. Yeah, we was posted up, kickin' it and getting perky and what have you. That was just a beautiful day.

In '94, me, him, Mac Mall, Spice 1, all of us got down on this song called "Dusted 'n' Disgusted" off of the EP *In a Major Way*. We were kickin' it, and he was rollin' up a Taylor, which is weed wrapped inside of a Zig Zag. We getting our perk on and Tupac gets a pen and paper. We got the beep blappin' and everything and he just goes at it and comes up with some of the coldest lyrics of all time with it. He killed it. We weren't rushing or nothing, he just wrote hecka quick. He wrote the verse in like ten minutes but it was cleaner than Clorox.

When he was locked up, I wrote him a letter and I told him I had a song called "One Love" dedicated to all the folks who are doing hard time in the pen, one of them ol' heartfelt songs, the ones that will make a gangster cry when you listen to it. He wrote me a letter back and was telling me that he was just in there jail'n and wanted to congratulate me on my newborn son. He also wrote that he had been seeing me on *Yo MTV Raps* and *Rap City* and told me that "One Love" was bangin'. He was able to see all that from in there.

We did this song called "Million Dollar Spot" off of the album *Tha Hall of Game* and when we did that he was working on his album also and was on some real nigga shit. I asked him what we gotta do about the business on this. He said, "Look, you just do one for me and I'll do one for you." I was like, damn, he a real muthafucka. I knew he was cut from the same cloth, from the same material or fabric that I was cut from. We don't care who is hot at the time, it doesn't matter. Forget the money, we don't gotta exchange no money. Like, you do something for me, I'll do something for you. I'll shoot you a verse, you shoot me a verse. And that is how Pac was. He was like that with the people that he felt.

We shot the video for "Rappers' Ball" with K-Ci from Jodeci and Too Short. We were in Calabasas at a mansion. It was all of us, Ice-T, Mack 10—we was all tycoonin', just getting prepared for the scenes and everything and Tupac comes in the trailer and asks us if we wanna hear some of his new shit. I said, "Hell yeah, put that muthafucka in." We started talking about our new handles. I told him mine was 40fonzerelli. He said, "Well I'm Makaveli." I thought to myself, "Makaveli? That sounds like Fonzerelli." Come to find out, he broke that shit down to me and let me know that Machiavelli was a real person and woo wop de woo and all the shit he did. And I was like, this nigga is incredible. He played that fuckin' "Hail Mary" and did this little dance to it too while we was in the trailer. He was killin' that shit. He had a bottle of Hennessy in his hand. I was like, this nigga is a damn *fool*.

That was the last time I saw my dude.

E-40isms

CAMPAIGNIN': Making your presence felt, showing off, out the sunroof or sitting on

the door panels of your convertible car and campaign like u running for president

FUNKIN': Beef, beefin', war, feuding

JAIL'N: Doing time in jail, waiting for release, programming, rolling with the punches

PERKIN': Under the influence of alcohol, tipsy drunk

POSTED UP: Posted on the block, to stand or set up shop at a certain spot

POW WOW: To conversate, talking to one another

SMELL ME: You feel me, do you understand what I'm saying?

THUMPERS: Handgun, a pistol

TYCOON: A top hat, someone wit lots of money

BLAPPIN': Trunk of the car throbbin' and vibrating, going blap, blap, blap

UPHELD YOUR BAYNESS: Represent yo city no matter where you're at

WOOP WOP, WOO WOP: Anything. Example— "hand me my woop wop, or woo wop"

TREACH

> Before Treach was a member of the platinum-selling hip-hop group Naughty by Nature, he and Tupac began their rise to stardom together as roadies in 1990.

I met Pac on the Public Enemy tour in 1990 when I was a roadie and performing with Queen Latifah. Tupac was a roadie and performing with Digital Underground. When we linked up, that was the start of the whole thing. We were road dogs. Every day we were together. The little money we had, we was out getting weed; messin' with the groupies. We were superstars of our own little ghetto. Nobody knew us, but we came on stage freestylin' and doing our thing in separate shows. It was something we had never experienced before. We were outside of the hood. We were hustling in a legal way. We weren't gonna get in

Treach, Tupac, and Eazy-E.

Treach showing off his Tupac tattoo.

trouble for what we were doin'. We was used to hustling on the streets. So we saw a whole new life together—from two different hoods, but like the same type of homies with the same mindset, looking for the same type of thing.

Tupac didn't have fear of what anybody thought. He didn't think, "Yo, somebody might feel this way if I say this." He felt that if he told you the truth without watering it down, you'd respect him and get a lot more out of it. Sometimes I'd be like, "Pac, shut up, these police are about to let us go." He'd say, "Fuck that, they got to understand."

There was so much Pac wanted to do and accomplish. He had the fire in his eye. What hurt him the most was people not understanding him and painting the picture of this bad guy. He was gonna grab the whole thug nation. Once he had it, he was going to take us from hip-hop to poetry to politics. It was in his blood to lead his people and help them overcome the oppression, and he knew the only way he could do it was to have the thugs behind him. That's how Thug Life came into existence. We were all the original Thug Life. He had people from everywhere, whether they were wearing red or blue. The Cyphers, Vice Lords, Latin Kings, it didn't matter, everybody is Thug Life. Once everybody was together and knew each other, there would be a whole different look on your face, and you can't kill 'em as easy.

He had all elements. He was a baby Panther. He was a soldier. He was a poet. He was a visionary. He was a thug. He was a prophet. We got robbed of someone who was gonna take us where we needed to be.

CHASING
LIFE

"Tupac stands out as a warrior. He was always fighting for a cause—to be free on the outside when in reality your freedom is inside. He was just dealing with so much. He was always making us understand that he was in the struggle with us. Through songs like 'Keep Your Head Up' and 'Brenda's Got a Baby,' he tells us the truth. He dealt with the truth. He touched on women having babies too young. He touched on a lot of women not being secure with themselves. That is why a lot of women liked him. He was always in the struggle for *us*. And he was the only man doing that. While everyone else was calling women bitches and hos, Pac was saying, 'Keep Your Head Up.'"
—Mary J. Blige

MAYA ANGELOU

> Maya Angelou—American poet, world-renowned author, and Civil Rights activist—took time to reach out to Tupac during an early period of his career, offering much-needed guidance and wisdom.

Years ago, I did a movie called *Poetic Justice*, and there was a young man, the first day, who cursed so! I couldn't believe it. I walked around behind him, tried to ignore him. But the second day, he and another young man, black man, ran to each other and they were about to fight and hundreds of extras started to run away, but one black man walked up to the two young men and I walked up. I took one by his shoulder, I said, "Let me speak to you." He said, "If these blah-blah . . . " I said, "Let me speak to you, honey." "Well, I tell you something, blah-blah . . . " I said, "No, let me talk to you, please." And he finally calmed down and I said, "Do you know how much you are needed? Do you know what you mean to us? Do you know that hundreds of years of struggle have been for you? Please, baby, take a minute. Don't lose your life on a zoom." I put my arm around him. He started to weep. The tears came down. That was Tupac Shakur. I took him, I walked him down into a little gully, and kept his back to the people so they wouldn't see him, and I used my hands to dry his cheeks. I kept talking to him sweetly, sweetly. For the next week while I was on that film, whenever I walked by, he would be saying, "So I told these . . . " —he would say, "Good morning, Ms. Angelou."

> Tupac's encounter with Maya Angelou affected him so deeply, he called his mother afterwards and described it to her. In turn, Afeni wrote Maya a thank-you note.

Thank you Older sister!
My son is Tupac Shakur.
You treated him as though
you knew he was one of yours;
as though he had been
raised by somebody.
I believe you poured
much needed water
on seeds which had
been planted in my son's
soul. Please keep teaching
till you can teach no
more — We need the
reinforcements in the
trenches — In Sisterly
gratitude

Excerpt from Afeni's thank-you letter to Maya Angelou.

KAREN LEE

> The first time Karen Lee and Tupac met was during a rally at the 168th Street Armory in New York, when he was just an infant. It wasn't until two decades later, when Karen Lee was hired by Interscope Records as Tupac's publicist, that their real relationship began.

One of the reasons that I loved Tupac so much was that I knew who and what he was inside. People thought he was like Bishop, the out-of-control and violent character he portrayed in *Juice*. His personality was actually closer to the sensitive and romantic character he portrayed in *Poetic Justice*. He definitely wasn't Bishop. He wasn't a murderer. He had a respect for life but a fear for what the future seemed to hold for so many young black men. His mother had raised him with a respect for women and people . . . especially people in under-served communities.

While on his first promo tour for *2pacalypse Now*, he was invited to speak at a dinner in Atlanta hosted by the Malcolm X Grassroots Movement. The first speaker was a professor from NYU who had been dismissed for being too controversial. He was an educated black man who spoke with knowledge and passion about black history and the African-American experience in America.

Not having heard Tupac speak publicly before, I was concerned about how he would handle following such an astute speaker. It was a concern I would never have again.

Pac got up and began to speak very passionately about the Panther Party, African Americans in America today and yesterday. He used some profanity while speaking. I saw a woman who was sitting next to him on the dais and I saw her discomfort with his language. Finally she leaned over and asked him to please "watch his language." Tupac looked down at her and said, in a respectful tone, "you can't be any more offended by my language than I am by the world that your generation left me to live in."

It was one of the many times that I was proud of him. He wasn't rude or arrogant. He continued talking about his mom, explaining how the Panther party had abandoned their family when his mother needed them the most. While Afeni and Tupac may have had numerous disagreements and separations, anyone who *really* knew him knew that he loved his mother fiercely. This evening marked the beginning of our relationship, which became more personal than professional for me.

In fact, I still have a photo that Pac autographed for me, saying "To my other mother, thanks for the eyes in the back of my head." That photo means the world to me. While I know the challenges that Afeni has faced over the years, I have always had a tremendous amount of respect for her. For Pac to consider me his "other mother" was one of the greatest compliments anyone has ever paid me.

I also remember having a Thanksgiving dinner at my home. Tupac and two of his friends came. There was an interesting mix of folks and I just stood back and watched some of my "intellectual" friends become mesmerized by how charismatic Pac was and how sweet. They left that dinner with an entirely new perspective about him . . . and the generation he represented.

The Christmas after *Juice* was released was very special. About midnight on Christmas Eve someone knocked on my door. It was Pac and his manager, Atron Gregory. He'd bought me a pair of diamond earrings and wanted his gift to be the first one I received on Christmas morning.

The sentiment touched my heart, and my soul, and those earrings still have a very special place in my jewelry box.

Several years later—after many shared experiences, both positive and negative— the sex abuse case in New York took center stage in Pac's life and the lives of those of us who loved him. I remember sitting in the office of one of the corporate attorneys for Time Warner with Atron Gregory and Tupac's manager Watani Tyehimba. The attorney asked us why there were no African-American leaders stepping forward to assist in this case.

Atron, Watani, and I looked at each other with no answer. There was no Jesse Jackson. No Al Sharpton. No Colin Powell. Nobody wanted to get involved with Tupac at that time. Pac was convicted of the equivalent of touching a woman's behind and he was being treated like a terrorist. No one even inquired as to whether or not he was guilty.

However, when he died, they called. They wanted to speak. I was personally disappointed that we had allowed the media to make us fear a young man who could have been destined for greatness. No one knew that "Red" would mature into Malcolm X. I didn't understand why no one saw the greatness that was inside Tupac. Well, they did see it, but it was after he was gone.

I do understand how difficult Pac could be, but he was a young man trying to find himself. When he was released from prison, he seemed to me to be out of control. When he returned to L.A., he called me and said he wanted to see me but was on his way to Mexico to go deep-sea fishing. I laughed and said, "Deep-sea fishing? You can't even swim." He laughed but there was something in that laugh that concerned me.

When he returned to L.A., I saw him driving down Sunset Boulevard, in a Rolls-Royce Cornish convertible smoking a blunt. I pulled up next to him and when he saw me shaking my head and smiling he pulled over, got out, and came over to give me a hug and a kiss. I chastised him about the blunt, reminding him that he was not free, but out on bail. He laughed and told me I worried too much but that he wanted to get together so I could hear some of the music he was working on and read some of the lyrics and scripts he had written while in prison.

Pac was chasing life, not living it. He talked about prison and death, sometimes carrying the possibility of both like a twin. I remember on his twenty-first birthday, while filming *Poetic Justice*, he said that he never thought he would reach twenty-one. He thought he'd be dead by that time.

There were so many memories. So many special times. So much love and now those memories are all that I have to cherish of him. He was a very special young man and I will forever have a large space in my heart for him and I thank God daily for sharing him with me.

WARREN G

> An unexpected phone call from Tupac brought rapper/producer Warren G to Echo Sound Studios late one night, where Tupac wrote and recorded two of his most acclaimed songs, "Definition of a Thug Nigga" and "How Long Will They Mourn Me?"

I remember the first time I heard Tupac. I was living in Long Beach, California, on 20th Street, doin' what I do, trying to survive. I heard his song "A Soldier's Story." It made me feel like nothing could hold me back. It gave me a rush—it made me feel like I was a youngster, and I needed to get out there and be a soldier about things. Tupac's songs always took me to a whole new zone. I could relate to everything he talked about 'cause I was going through a lot of that same stuff. It was amazing to me. I was like, "Damn! This nigga, we on the same page. This nigga's like my brother, he knows what I'm going through."

I met him around 1992. I was living with my sister on Cedar Street, sleeping on her floor, when he called her house. He said, "Warren, you did that Indo smoke beat?" I was like, "Yeah, I did that." He was like, "Well, I need a beat." I woke up out of my sleep. I asked him where he was, and he said Echo Sound Studios. I grabbed my heat—I had a .45. I grabbed my little bag, wrapped up my mixer and my turntable, and jumped into my raggedy-ass Regal.

I walked into the studio and he started asking me what was up. It went on for a while— he just kept asking me what was up with me. I told him a lot of stuff I was going through, how I didn't have any money, and how I felt I was struggling just to get some money to eat, and how I was left for dead 'cause I wasn't with Snoop and Dre and Death Row, and how I felt down and out. I told him I was having shoot-outs in the hood with niggas and shit. Right after that he said, "Warren, let me get a beat." So I loaded my shit up and I played him one of my tracks. He grabbed a pad and started writing and bouncing and shit. He had a beanie with the little string hangin' down, and a blunt in his mouth, and then he started singing the hook from "Definition of a Thug Nigga." When he went in the vocal booth, he was talking about everything that I'd just told him. That guy is incredible.

During that same session Big Syke came in, and Little Syke, and Mack 10, and Rated R. They came into the studio and told Pac that his homeboy Kato had got smoked in Detroit.

He was kind of fucked up after that. Some girls came in and everybody was fucked up and huggin' and shit. He asked, "Warren, you got a beat for that? I wanna do a song about my homeboy." So I threw up the beat for the song, "How Long Will They Mourn Me?" and he rapped about his homeboy Kato on the song. "Definition of a Thug Nigga" and "How Long Will They Mourn Me?" were two classics we did together. I had a great experience with him in the studio, those hours we were together. We hooked up again in other sessions, but it was never like that.

> "How Long Will They Mourn Me?" was on Tupac's third album, *Thug Life*, which reached #6 on *Billboard*'s Top R&B/Hip Hop albums.

> "Definition of a Thug Nigga" was on *R U Still Down*, which reached platinum status in 1997.

RUSSELL SIMMONS

> It was inevitable that Tupac's path would cross with that of hip-hop pioneer and business mogul Russell Simmons. But nobody could have guessed that it was Russell's endorsement of Tupac that would secure his role of Spoon in *Gridlock'd*.

I saw Tupac start to rise, and met him around the time of "Brenda's Got a Baby." But I didn't really get to know him well until he moved to New York to make the movie *Bullet* with Mickey Rourke. I knew Mickey, so I started to hang around Tupac more often. Then I made the movie *Gridlock'd* with him, and got to know him a lot better on the set. I wouldn't say that I was a great friend of his, but I really got to know that he had a lot of character. If Tupac walked into a room, everyone would notice. The whole room would be his. He had a great presence.

When I'd see Tupac in a violent or rough setting, like some places uptown and in Queens, he'd always be so comfortable in it. Then I'd see him in the settings of New York's social elite. I remember Christy Turlington threw an event for El Salvador, a benefit where everybody dressed in black tie. Tupac came in, and was so eloquent. He fit every environment. The same with his records—he could move the whole spectrum. He was a chameleon. He's always gonna have a presence. They're gonna teach his poetry fifty years from now at UCLA. He's a great poet and he's one of the people who defines our time. He's not going anywhere. There's not gonna be any lack of Tupac airplay or lack of material just because he's not here.

There are people who define the times from a cultural standpoint. They tell you which car is hot, which watch we wanna wear today. They offer a great kind of insight into a specific week or year. Tupac did that at times, but he also defined the spirit of something that's timeless. His songs were timeless. Until you end poverty or until you end suffering, you're always gonna need a Tupac song to describe what's really inside you.

Once we sat at the Bowery Bar downtown all night and talked about New York and how it was influencing him. He'd work in and he would see these threatening places, but he'd also see that a short drive or short subway ride away would lead to a less threatening place. It was kind of lightening up his heart a little bit. Allowing him to grow as a person. He was starting to appreciate the whole world, instead of the more difficult part of the world. The same kind of transformation hit him in Hollywood while he was making movies—he saw the "rest of the world" more often than not. It was where he had to be for business and it gave him opportunity.

Tupac is exactly like kids who don't have his worldwide platform, who lose their lives to violence or to drugs. He is a child who exemplifies what happens when we don't pay attention to giving people opportunities, education, and a sense of belonging in society. Tupac is an example of the kids we have to protect.

JAMAL JOSEPH

> The youngest member of the Panther 21 and a close friend of Afeni's, "Uncle Jamal" became someone who Tupac not only sought advice from, but also someone with whom he enjoyed long, intellectual conversations about his life and career. During difficult years for Tupac—when he survived five shots in an ambush in New York, a felony trial and conviction, and a prison term—Jamal stood by.

When he was little he had this great laugh. His laugh would make you want to grab him and tickle him, just to get that laugh and that energy.

He used to ride his little tricycle through the house, yelling "Out of the way! Out of the way!" Of course, he thought it was his motorcycle, and he was wearing his racing helmet. And I remember seeing him at Afeni's job while she worked at South Bronx Legal Services. She'd set him up at a desk and he'd color or do his homework while Afeni worked. I'd ask him if he was going to be a lawyer. He'd say, "Yeah, maybe, Uncle Jamal."

As a child, Tupac was the one who never quit. I used to have a karate school called the Black Cipher, and I was his instructor. When he was about eight or nine years old, he'd want to spar with me and the bigger kids. One time he sparred with this kid who was about twelve. The kid hit him hard with a kick, and I told Tupac to bow. He kept saying, "No, Sensei, I gotta finish the match." His blood was dripping on the mat, but he was determined to keep going. He had this incredible spirit and light in his eyes. He was always the most enthusiastic kid in the class.

Years later, the night after Tupac got shot in New York, I went over to the hospital to see him. There were fans outside, police, and hospital security guards. I was trying to get through, and Afeni's sister Glo saw me and told the guards to let me in. They gave the family a small waiting room, which was populated with about thirty people: members from the Shakur family, security, Tupac's manager Atron, Interscope Records people, and a few older Muslim guys. But everybody was connected as part of the family and extended family. People were going in shifts to see Tupac, because the hospital would only allow a few visitors at a time. I was next to go up to see him, when I heard someone say, "Here comes Tupac." I thought to myself, "What do they mean, here comes Tupac?" And sure enough, here he was, limping off the elevator with Afeni. We got him into a wheelchair, and Tupac was saying, "Get me out of here. They crazy, they tried to kill me. I wanna get out of here." A few people tried to talk him out of leaving, and then Afeni asked me to try. I kneeled over and put my forehead against his and said, "Pac. Man, you're shot. You're bleeding." He said, "Uncle Jamal, I don't care. They're crazy. You can take me somewhere else. Just get me out of here."

Calls were made to a friend who was a doctor, and she agreed to come see him at another location. By then the hospital security and the police figured out what was going on, and came into the family waiting room area. A hospital police officer came over to tell us that we couldn't take him out of the hospital. I said, "Sir, please look around you. You got former Panthers, you have some street soldiers. You have the fruit of Islam. Don't tell us we can't take him out. Show us where we can sign him out. And we would appreciate it if you would take us by the back entrance so we can get by the fans."

We took him to a friend's apartment. The next day, he was bleeding and having some problems. But he was strong—he wasn't even taking pain meds. At one point he may have smoked a little weed. He wasn't somebody to lay in the dark and moan about the pain. People had to make him rest. He would sit up in bed, talking on the regular phone and talking on the cell phone, making sure things were moving. That's just how he was.

A month later, I visited him at the Bellevue Prison ward. Tupac came out in a prison jumpsuit. He had a slight limp and moved a little slowly, but he looked good for having been shot five times just a month, or six weeks, before. He looked like he was gaining a little weight, and getting his cuts back. We hugged and sat down on opposite sides of the table. He said, "Uncle Jamal, before you start I wanna tell you a story." He said, "Man, they brought this guy into the prison ward from upstate. When I came in, he jumped up and ran over to me and said, 'What's up, Dog? I love you, man. Tupac, man, you're my hero. You are my hero, man.' I said, 'Wait a minute. Time out. Why am I your hero?' He said, 'Come on, Pac, are you kiddin'? You be getting all the bitches, getting paid. You be shootin' at the police.'"

Pac then told the guy, "Time out, if that's why I'm your hero then I don't need to be anyone's hero." Tupac told me that at that moment he knew the Thug Life thing needed to die. He also said that he knew that he was gonna die. He said, "I'm a Shakur, they have to kill me. But the thing is, man, do I wanna go out like Malcolm X, or do I just wanna go out like any thug gangster?" He told me that day that he wanted to die like Malcolm X.

I assured him he wasn't going to die, and then we took the conversation to his beautiful, powerful vision to start youth centers in every city, in every urban center. He was gonna get artists to give money and time to the kids. The centers were going to be liberation and art schools, similar to the Panther's Liberation schools of the '70s. It was an exciting day for me. I disregarded all the talk about him dying and focused on his vision for these schools.

One of our ongoing debates was about Thug Life. He'd told me several months before the Bellevue visit that Thug Life was going to be a movement. I asked him why he was talking about Thug Life when he was a Panther child. Huey Newton and Bobby Seal were thugs and they became revolutionaries. Malcolm X was a thug and then became a revolutionary. George Jackson was a thug and then he became a revolutionary. "You were born a revolutionary," I said. "Why are you stepping backwards?"

Tupac responded, "It's kind of like the teachings in Islam that God meets you at the point of your will. Well, I gotta keep it real with the niggas that kept it real with me. I gotta meet them at the point of their will."

I responded to him by saying, "Pac, every now and then, the Creator gives someone the voice to speak to and for their whole generation, and you are that voice for this generation. You have their ear and their hearts. You can change the world." And he did!

> A month after Tupac's death, Jamal co-founded a creative arts youth program in Harlem named "Impact," which was inspired by Tupac's vision of bringing arts, education, and activism to young people. In 2000, Jamal brought his "Impact" kids to the Tupac Amaru Shakur Center for the Arts in Atlanta to teach their methods to the counselors and students.

JASMINE GUY

> After Tupac was shot in New York, he became convinced he was a target, and left the hospital before being officially released. He took refuge in the apartment of his friend Jasmine Guy, an actress and one of the stars of *A Different World*.

We used to talk about so many different things. Tupac used to say, "That's legend, put that in the book." It drove me nuts. I used to say, "*You* put that in the book." And then I'd think, "Why does he always say that? I'm not writing any book about him."

One thing he often talked about was how he felt abandoned. He would tell me stories about how when he was younger he lived with different friends for a few weeks at a time, and what that felt like. He got mad at me once for telling him that my parents' divorce was such an emotional and painful turning point in my life. His response was, "At least your parents were together for twenty-three years. You should be happy you had twenty-three years with your parents. I don't even know my father."

He listened to his friends intently. And he remembered *everything*. I can't believe he could remember things with all that weed he smoked. I'd say to him, "I'm glad your brain still works."

In acting, he'd remember his lines just like that. I'd have to study and study my lines. But he'd just read his in the trailer, and then go out and do it. He had a brilliant mind.

When Tupac was shot in New York, Jada and I flew in from L.A. I went there to support Tupac, but also because Jada needed support, too. I didn't want her to be alone. I had an apartment in New York, and when Tupac left the hospital, he stayed on my couch.

I understood what he was feeling. He was so conflicted, and trying to deal with the betrayal of the shooting. His friends were driving him nuts.

His family was there of course, and even though it was my house, I felt like I was an intruder, so I would leave them alone a lot. This was such an intense time for their family, and they were very close. Tupac and I were friends, but it wasn't my place to intrude.

They also *wanted* to keep me out of it. They were very protective about that. There was no other sanctuary for him. I was trustworthy, but I wasn't in that world he lived in. My friends weren't his friends, and I think Pac's family wanted to keep it that way. If that privacy was gone, then they'd have to go somewhere else. Because his world was kept so much

A Polaroid taken at the Clinton Correctional Facility.

at bay, it made us all able to just concentrate on him. He had all these holes in his body and it was just a very horrific time to be trying to deal with the outside world.

While he stayed at my place, he read all of my books. He was an avid reader, but it's almost like he didn't want people to know that. He wanted a certain image. Sometimes, I'd feel like I knew a whole different person. I'd read a *Vibe* article and think, "That doesn't sound like him." But that was just Pac. He could relate to a lot of different kinds of people.

I think one thing it's important to know about Pac was that he was able to have long-term relationships and friendships with women. And that he still means so much to his friends. If he were just screwing around with these women, people wouldn't remember that. That's not stuff you cry about after someone is gone. You're sad that you can't talk to him anymore. You think to yourself, "What about that movie? What about the book he was gonna write? What about his future, his dreams, his center? What about the charity benefit he was gonna do?"

Tupac and Afeni brought rich gifts to my life, just by letting me into their circle. They're like a clan, and you don't let just anyone into a clan; they're protective and posses-sive about who they let inside. So I thought that after Pac was better and back on his feet, I wouldn't see them anymore. I even called Tupac's aunt Glo when he left, and had this whole good-bye conversation with her, letting her know how much they all meant to me. I'd had such great conversations with the women in Pac's family while he stayed with me. Glo said, "What are you talking about? Where are we going?" We stayed very close, and Afeni and Glo are still there.

> In 2004, Jasmine Guy authored Afeni's life story, *Evolution of a Revolutionary*, and has honored Tupac with her work at the Tupac Amaru Shakur Center for the Arts, where she has taught acting workshops.

IRIS CREWS

> Though Tupac had numerous legal battles, the sexual abuse charge he went to prison for upset him the most deeply and caused him to feel a great betrayal. Iris Crews, one of Tupac's attorneys in the case, only knew him for a short time in his life, but it was a pivotal time.

As a law student I had gone to court to help with the case of Mutulu Shakur. Several years after Mutulu was convicted, the Tupac case came to order in the New York City courts. I was asked by Mutulu and Tupac's attorney Michael Warren to sit as co-counsel. I didn't know much about Tupac; I'd heard some of his music, but didn't know who he was as an individual. After I realized the nature of the case and the nature of the charges, I told Michael that I couldn't represent the brother until I talked to him.

I remember when they were going into court for a preliminary hearing. We were outside, and Tupac was in a van with his entourage. He was sleeping. So they said to me, "Come on, you can meet him now." I went to the van and I heard someone tell him, "Tupac, wake up, your attorney's here." He was very groggy and he said something like, tell her I'll meet her another time. I said to myself, "Oh really?" I wasn't going to tolerate that, nor would I represent someone who felt that way about me as an attorney.

I told Michael that I can't represent anyone that I don't believe in. I told him we can do it this evening or even another day, but I have never even had a conversation with him. So they made an arrangement for me to meet with Tupac privately. I didn't want his entourage, just me and him. So we went to a place in Brooklyn called the River Cafe, just he and I, and we talked. We talked about the young lady [who was accusing him of sexual abuse], we talked about the incident. He told me what had happened, and more importantly, he showed me the respect I needed to continue on with the case, 'cause I had to be able to look in his eyes and believe this young man. I had to listen to his voice and believe him. He opened doors for me. He pulled out my chair. I didn't get that bravado stuff—I didn't get all of that cursing. I got a very, very different person. And I learned he was somebody quite different than the person shown on TV. I knew he was somebody I could represent and work with.

He was afraid. I got that in his voice. He was hurt. He thought that he had been betrayed and he said so to me. He said, "I respect women, and for someone to do this to me, to set me up like this, hurts me." So from that moment on, from that day on, every day we got to court if he saw me and he was sitting down, he would stand up. I think Tupac wanted discipline. He wanted structure. When we first started the trial, he would come into court with the big T-shirt and the baggy jeans, and I told him that I wasn't gonna sit next to him if he had that on. I told him that he had to come to court prepared, that he was a warrior in this setting and that he had to wear warrior clothes.

After he got shot, he was staying in Manhattan and all of us went to see him. He was on a couch and his leg was stretched out. When he saw me, he got right up. He stood up with his bad leg. You know, that's the kind of respect that he had in him to give someone.

Tupac was a prolific reader. During the trial he'd buy newspapers and read them in between court sessions. He'd read the *Daily News* and the *Post*, which surprised me because the *Post* is such a racist paper. Sometimes he'd read the *Times*. And he used to sit in court and write on his legal pad. One day he wrote down some poetry of Robert Frost's. I looked at what he was writing and said, "Give me that," because I was so surprised. He would always be reading in the hallways when we were in court between sessions. And there were always children from his family around, and he would tell me, "See these kids here, they rely on me." So that was the responsibility that this young man felt from the age of nineteen, twenty, twenty-one years old, not just for his sister, but all the kids from his extended family.

After Tupac was convicted, the judge gave him a certain time to surrender. We felt that if he surrendered early, in a few hours, it would be good and it would look better on his behalf. We went to this apartment and there were a lot of people there; I knew that if he had his people with him, we'd get a very different response. I was the only woman there, and I asked the other two male attorneys if I could talk to Tupac alone, because I knew I'd get a different reaction from him. I take none of the credit here, but the Creator gave me the words to say what I had to say to him at that time.

At first Tupac said no. He kept saying, "I'm not going to jail. I'm not gonna do that [surrender]." He said, "Look what happened to Mutulu. I'm not gonna have the same thing happen to me. I'm not gonna spend my life in jail. I'm not gonna do it." So I just let him talk. And then I hugged him and said, "Tupac, we're gonna do this. All of us are gonna do this together. We're gonna watch out for you and we're gonna protect you. It's gonna be all right." But he kept saying he wasn't gonna surrender. He felt that he'd rather die or escape. He'd rather flee the jurisdiction.

I knew he was afraid. God, we were all afraid.

And finally he agreed.

BIG SYKE

> Of all Tupac's friends, it was Big Syke who gave him the deepest insight into L.A. gangs. When Tupac was released from prison, it was Big Syke who was there to greet him.

I met Tupac when he was recording *Strictly 4 My N.I.G.G.A.Z.* He said he wanted to start this thing called Thug Life and I was like, "I'm with it." It was something I wanted to be a part of, 'cause when he said "Thug," it was like "uh-huh, that sounds like me." That kind of helped me find myself, 'cause I used to be a gangster, you know, but I found out I ain't no gangster, I'm just a thug.

The number one thing I tried to tell Pac was that the Crips and the Bloods and everybody else loved him. So he had the opportunity to squash a lot of beef, 'cause everybody wanted to deal with him. Everybody liked him. So that's what I was trying to push ahead . . . to keep it real.

I always gave Pac the credit of a G in the music business. I never looked at him as no street G. I looked at him as my little homeboy, somebody who'd be doing crazy stuff that he really didn't need to be doing. And that right there is where we used to bump heads, when I used to try to tell him, "Hey, calm down because something is gonna happen." He'd say, "I don't give a fuck. Fuck that!" He tried to act like I was scared. So I'm like, "Nigga, I ain't no buster 'cause I know what's gonna happen. Calm down or we gonna be dead. Ain't no pluses in that shit."

I remember when he asked me if he should sign with Death Row Records. I thought there was something funny about it, because Pac just had a double platinum album. He should've had the money sittin' up at Interscope for them to bail him out of Dannemora. I believe that Interscope thought that Suge [Knight] was gonna control him. But how can you control a piece of dynamite? You can't. 'Cause it's already lit. So what they did was put Suge in, got some more gunpowder with the already lit stick of dynamite. Everything's gonna just blow up even bigger now. But he *signed* . . . on a *napkin*. Signed to get five million for three albums.

Whatever Tupac did, he maximized that shit. He got a little taste of Thugism from me and just ran with it. Shit, all my grades in school was damn near F's and D's. I did time when I was fifteen years old. I ain't been to no ballet. I just knew something was different

Tupac and Big Syke (in blue on right) with others.

about this nigga. This nigga knew too many damn words. But that's what I got from him. Thugs need to read books, man. 'Cause he made these cats wonder, who the hell is Machiavelli? He named me "Mussolini," so I had to go grab a book and read up on this fool.

When he was spittin', he would mix up big-ass words into some gangster shit, and it had me sayin', *damn*. That nigga said, "I was so optimistic." I said, "What the fuck did that nigga say?" At the time I didn't know what optimistic meant. I'd go get my thesaurus and say, "What the hell this nigga say?" He was a living thesaurus.

He was also known for some politician-type shit. This nigga was running around makin' a movement. Changing shit. So that's what I think he gave the blacks, especially the youth. You know words are powerful. And the more of them you know, the better you gonna be.

GOBI

> Tupac was known for his cutting-edge, push-the-envelope music videos. Video producer
Gobi was both witness and accomplice to Tupac's work on the set.

The first video my partner Tracy Robinson and I produced for Tupac was "How Do U Want
It?" The X-rated, R-rated version. I just remember seeing a lot of naked girls on set and
hearing that Tupac had asked the crew to take their shirts off 'cause he wanted the girls to
feel more comfortable. It was hilarious to watch all these crew people walking around with
no shirts on. The crew was mostly men, and the girls were all strippers and porn stars. I
mean, that's a small price to pay to see naked women walking around all over the place.

It was an elaborate set. What was really cool about Pac's vision was that he didn't like
doing what was expected. He always wanted to do something out of the box. Like one of the
rooms as a period piece. One as futuristic, you know, and he liked all the role reversals here,
he liked strong women and submissive men. He did a lot of that sort of stuff. He was a big
praiser, but he also had a very, very short fuse and liked things to be done yesterday. If they
weren't, he would lose his cool.

My first directing job after producing a number of videos was Tupac's "2 of Amerikaz
Most Wanted." I remember it was a three-day shoot. The second day we were at Club Vagate
on La Cienega and there was a scene where Pac and Snoop were sitting in a little alcove. It
was like a little Denny's kind of thing. The two of them were sitting there and they were
singing the chorus. Pac was counting hundreds. They were real hundreds . . . always had to
be real hundreds, real Cristal, and real weed.

On the third day of the shoot after we shot one scene in the courtroom, Pac turned to
me and said, "Gobi, I'm done."

I said, "What are you talking about?"

He said "I'm done, you got a video."

I said, "Wait—we got a lot more to shoot."

He said, "Uh-uh, you've got enough. I'm out of here."

So he and Snoop got into their car and just took off and that was it. That was the end
of the video shoot. He worked in films and knew what the pace of shooting a film was, but
when we did music videos, he expected the pace of music videos to be ten times quicker.

Gobi and Tupac discussing a video shoot.

Tupac waiting for the set-up of a video shoot.

He would do a music video, a film, and the studio all in one twenty-four-hour period. His pace was unreal. Tracy and I produced and directed six big videos for him all in a couple of months. He wanted his own production company, his own people, his own movies, and his own music. He wanted autonomy. But it felt like the powers around him didn't want that. So there was this tug of war going on.

One of the last conversations I had with him, he said, "You know, in six months or a year from now, people aren't going to recognize me, 'cause I'm gonna act like such an adult." He said, "I'm gonna be so mature and, in fact, you know what? I'm going to put all this bullshit aside and one day I might even go for politics. I might even run for mayor of Los Angeles 'cause these politicians are the biggest corrupt gangsters in the business."

He was funny. He was ridiculous at times. He used to call me his crazy Iranian. What I miss most about Tupac is his no-limit approach to life. Having him in my life taught me about endless possibilities. I really wish I could have seen a glimpse of what he was on his way to becoming. I wish the world could have seen it.

KEVIN POWELL

> Kevin Powell, a former senior writer for *Vibe* magazine, wrote what are widely considered the definitive articles on Tupac Shakur when he was alive. Powell was not only a journalist, in Tupac's eyes, but also a friend. While most writers spent their time reporting on Tupac's legal troubles, Kevin spent his time trying to expose all of Tupac's dimensions.

When *Vibe* magazine was started in 1992, it became hugely successful. Treach from Naughty by Nature, a friend of Tupac's, was on the very first cover, and I had written that story. We had an editorial meeting in the spring of '93, and different writers on the team dis-cussed who we wanted to write about. I said there was someone named Tupac Shakur I was interested in. I'd seen him in *Juice* the year before, and was blown away by his performance. He was an incredibly talented actor. Not to mention that I knew his music. I was always fascinated by artists who talked about socially conscious stuff, like he did with "Brenda's Got a Baby." But the *Vibe* editors didn't really know who Tupac was. I told them there was another reason I wanted to write about him; I'd been a political activist since I was eighteen years old, and the Shakur name was famous in black political circles. I knew about his mother Afeni and the whole Black Panther Party affiliation. But still the editors were kind of lukewarm about it.

In '92 and '93, the big hip-hop acts were Dr. Dre, Snoop Dogg, and Naughty by Nature. Tupac wasn't well known yet. But I knew he was representative of young black men in America. I told them that this was the young man who represents the hip-hop community, and that his was definitely a voice that they needed to check for. But the editors still didn't see my vision. I wanted to write a piece that positioned Tupac as the hip-hop James Dean—that's how much *Juice* had affected me. It made me think about the work of James Dean in the 1950s and how *Rebel Without a Cause* affected a lot of white sisters and brothers in the rock 'n' roll era.

I ended up meeting Tupac at the Jack the Rapper conference in Atlanta. I had heard he was gonna be there, and went with some folks from *Vibe* magazine. By this point, it was known that Kevin wanted to interview Tupac. So we were in the hotel lobby and he's over there and there's a lot of young ladies checkin' him out, and they're oohin' and aahin' and everything, so I was like, I'm not gonna go sweat this dude. And the lady I was with ended up going over to Tupac and telling him, "You need to know Kevin Powell." Tupac turned around and said, "Yo, you my man. I had your back on that show. I had your back." He knew me from being on MTV's very first season of *The Real World*. So here I was, nervous to meet Tupac, but turns out he was as happy to meet me as I was to meet him; 1992 was when *The Real World* aired, and it was also the year that Tupac came out in *Juice*. And it was also the year that *Vibe* magazine launched. So we were both all of a sudden thrust into this pop culture, two young black males.

Something happened around the time that I met him, I don't know whether it was when he was charged with assaulting the Hughes brothers or charged with the shooting incident with the police officers in Atlanta, but suddenly my editors were like, "Ummm. You still wanna do that article on Tupac?" It turned into the cover story, where Tupac was wearing a straightjacket and the caption was something like "Is Tupac Crazy?" And that really pissed me off because I did not want him categorized like that. But I couldn't say much after all, because Tupac posed for that picture. But that was Pac, he was a Gemini, and so he would do stuff like that, and give people the rope to do this kind of thing. But in that first article what I tried to do was really contextualize everything, because by the time the article came out, the media was trying to beat him up bad. So suddenly he's famous for his music, but more for getting in trouble.

He was so articulate, so intelligent. He was obviously a very handsome cat. He had an allegiance to his fans, but he also had this allegiance to the streets. He appealed to a lot of different people. And that's what I tried to capture in that first piece I wrote about him. For that first article, I interviewed him in Atlanta, we did stuff in L.A., walked around the community of South Central. You just saw someone who was at ease with all different types of people. He could talk to the educators and the principal of a school, but he could talk to the heads who were just standing outside eating some ribs at a soul food joint. I felt like my job was to capture the essence of who he truly was. And I remember one time he said to me, "I want you to be the Alex Haley to my Malcolm X."

When I interviewed him when he was locked up in Rikers Island, it was me and Tupac in the room, but there were also like ten other people: correctional officers, publicists, the photographer. But when Pac started talking, it was like there was no one else in the room. He was smoking a cigarette, finishing all his sentences with "Woop dee woo." I can still hear his voice right now; he was nervous and animated. He was describing the first time he got shot, and making circles with his cigarettes. There was complete silence in the room while he told the story and it took like two, three hours. Pac was a gifted storyteller.

I found out that Tupac was very angry with the way the interview came out. We had changed the names of some of the people he'd talked about. And to be honest with you, we changed the names because we wanted to protect Pac's life; he was calling people out. And we were like, that's not a smart move to call people out. Think about it—he'd been shot five times and the New York heads were saying all kinds of stuff about him. *Vibe* felt that it was necessary to change some names because you can't just accuse people of stuff when you have no proof of it. We could've gotten sued. What did bother me, though, was that *Vibe*, behind my back, allowed some of the folks that were in the recording studio the night that Pac got shot to rebut Tupac's interview. Tupac lumped all of us together and that was the end of our relationship, because it looked like I was down with what *Vibe* did, and that was not the case.

So Pac gets out of jail. And now *Vibe* wants to do a whole Death Row story. I remember I really didn't want to touch it 'cause I was kind of disgusted with where things were going. As a journalist you report what's going on, and I felt like the whole West Coast–East Coast thing was spiraling out of control. I asked myself if I really wanted to be a part of this. But it was too compelling to pass on. Because Suge was telling us the reporter could talk to him, to Dre, to Tupac, to Snoop, to Danny Boy. So we went out to the set of the "California Love" video shoot. I hadn't seen Tupac since he got out of jail. When I opened the door to his trailer, a gust of marijuana smoke came out. Now mind you, this was the same Tupac who told me a year before during the Rikers Island interview that he wasn't gonna smoke anymore, that he wasn't gonna drink anymore, that he was gonna change. And now he's wilder than ever. I was just like, damn, this is deep.

He was real distant and cold. So we went from, "Yo, you my man, I had your back," and me getting cool with his mother and sister, to that—distant and cold. So I knew that our relationship had changed. It was very sad. And that was the last time I saw him in person. I didn't even get to interview him that day.

I tried to interview him at Can Am Studios a week or so later. But he wasn't there. So I had to do a phone interview with him the next day. I asked him what was up with the East Coast–West Coast thing. And he sounded like a child when he answered. He said "Well, green M&M's and yellow M&M's don't go together." And this, the son of Afeni Shakur. This is a man who grew up with the stepfather Mutulu Shakur. This is a man who made songs like "Brenda's Got a Baby" and "Keep Ya Head Up." But Tupac had two personalities. One was really about the people. He was serious and socially conscious. And then the other part was not able to turn that corner. That was the last time he and I talked.

I followed Tupac from a distance after that. And I began to feel a tinge of jealousy when I would see other writers interviewing him. But I knew people were writing about him now in a sensationalistic aspect. And I felt that I'd developed this bond with him over the years because I took journalism very seriously and I wanted to balance the mainstream depictions of folks. I wanted to talk about the fact that Tupac read books, he could talk about all kinds of artists, from visual arts to theater—but they always made him one-dimensional. And I felt like in the last year of his life, he participated in that one-dimensionality.

I was sent to Las Vegas by *Rolling Stone* magazine after Tupac got shot the second time. I had been fired by *Vibe* earlier in the year. After Tupac's death was announced, I went to the corner where he was shot and I poured some liquor out the way that folks from the hood do, and I cried. I was just distraught. I felt guilty that I had basically stopped talking to the dude. When I got the phone call that let me know that he was gone, that was one of the saddest days of my life. And to this day I have not gone back to Vegas.

I think Tupac would've been one of the greatest actors of our generation. I think if he were still here they'd have been talking about Tupac Shakur in the way they talk about Leonardo DiCaprio and Matt Damon. I think he would have created an amazing body of music. I think he not only would've become a great actor, but also he would have become a great director. He had that in him and would've become a serious player in the film industry. I definitely think he would have been writing books. Politically he would have been someone like Harry Belafonte, Susan Sarandon, Sean Penn, or Barbra Streisand, who understood the power of their celebrity but who also have a high level of social consciousness. He would've used that to weigh in on important issues of the day because that's what he was doing all along.

I make my living speaking all over the country. I'm a political cat. I go to colleges, universities, churches, prisons, mosques, synagogues, community centers. You name it, I've been there. *Everywhere* I go, people ask me about Tupac. People have handed me copies of their dissertations to get their Ph.D. on Tupac. People are teaching courses at the high school level on Tupac. In New Hampshire this young white brother had his jacket open so I could see that he had on a Tupac T-shirt. They know me as the guy who interviewed Tupac. It's profound. I had no idea it was gonna be like that. Even in his death, he's still alive.

TALIB KWELI

> Talib Kweli, who just released his sixth album, is a socially conscious artist who is known for the purpose and depth in his music.

The first time I learned about Tupac I was at Summit Junior High in New York City. The host at Video Music Box, Ralph McDaniels, used to play all the cutting-edge music videos and since there wasn't any hip-hop on MTV yet, that was my source for hip-hop music.

Digital Underground had a song on the *Nothing But Trouble* soundtrack and Tupac was on the song. I was already a fan of Digital Underground, but Tupac's rhyme pattern and delivery was different than most West Coast groups. Then, in "Same Song," the fact that he was wearing African garb caught my attention.

Years later I met Tupac briefly at the Naughty by Nature video that Spike Lee directed, "Hip-Hop Hooray."

I saw him again after that at John Forte's birthday party with Biggie. I was with Knowledge from Digable Planets. We were at this nightclub called Country Club and Tupac and Biggie were trying to talk to these girls that I used to hang out with—so they all came by the table and we were drinking and smoking and partying together.

His albums are incredible. Him being an artist who grew up with the Black Panther movement, he spoke directly to me. My music is very much based in black history, the history of our people, particularly over the last thirty years. Tupac is a direct result of that and for him to become the most prolific artist of our time speaks to the power of that community.

On his albums, all his rhetoric, as angry and as fiery as it may be, is really a means to an end. It's really him reaching out to those dudes and those people that society has forgotten. And Tupac realized that if he spoke their language he had a shot at reaching them. Tupac's music was like listening to a hip-hop version of "48 Laws of Power." Because it was really about a total power, *by any means necessary* and using a language and using things that are negative to try to create a more positive outlook.

Now you have a whole generation of artists who take that template and use it. Tupac became the perfect model for being the perfect rapper.

PRESTON HOLMES

> Preston Holmes produced two of the four films that Tupac starred in, and became a close friend of the family after Tupac was killed. Preston later went on to produce the Oscar-nominated documentary *Tupac: Resurrection*.

I first met Tupac when he came along with Money B from Digital Underground, when Money B was auditioning for *Juice*. The casting director came out to the waiting area and took a look at the people and asked Tupac if he wanted to audition, too. Tupac said yes. Afterwards the director, Ernest Dickerson, and the casting director came to me and said, "We just found this incredible kid, he'll be great." He told me how it had all come about, how Tupac wasn't even one of the people that they'd called in that day and how amazing he was. Then I got the chance to meet him.

I got to know him while we shot *Juice* in New York. I was told he was a rapper, but I certainly wasn't aware of his work at that time. What I remember is how over the course of shooting the film, we all—myself and the crew—could see every day just how good this kid was. It was a tough film to make. We had a fairly low budget and a grueling shooting schedule, but when we'd watch the dailies, he was just brilliant. The other cast members were all veterans; Tupac was the exception. He was also the exception in another way. He was the only actor in the cast who was in every scene. He had to work every day, which meant he had a five or six a.m. call time and worked for fifteen or sixteen hours. What I realized after a couple weeks of shooting was that Tupac had been running with his crew at night, hanging out and probably working, recording, writing, or whatever. He was not sleeping. Granted he was a young man, but that would take a toll on anyone. But he was there every day, always prepared, always brilliant.

I remember one instance when he was complaining to me about how his back hurt and how tired he was. I made some comment about him being too young to be tired. He told me, "This is y'all's thing. I'm not into all this. My thing is my music." I said, "That may be. But from what I've seen, when this movie comes out, that will all change." I think at the time he really felt his music career was taking off, which of course it did, immediately.

I was talking to one of the other actors from *Juice* the week that Tupac was in the hospital in Vegas, and he said that he and another main character in *Juice* felt that after the movie came out, Tupac had decided to in some ways have Bishop become his public face, because of the way people responded to that character in the movie. I don't know how true that is, but it wouldn't surprise me because everything that Tupac did was calculated. And I think he was actor enough to be anything he wanted to be, or felt it was necessary to be. For instance, when he was at Death Row years later, I thought he was out-Death-Row-ing the Death Row people. He became the face of Death Row. Wherever he went, people fed off his energy and passion, and that's why he was always out front.

When he was in jail years later, I wrote to Tupac and told him that I had moved to L.A. to run a new film company, Def Pictures. I knew he was going to be released soon and I told him, "I know that you have stories to tell and I'd like to help you do that." He wrote back, "Good lookin' out—but not only do I have stories to tell, I have a script. I wrote it since I've been here and I'd like for you to take a look at it." I also told him that I had a script for him, *Gridlock'd*. Tupac read the script and loved it. But Polygram had some problems with Tupac. The head of the company, Michael Kuhn, asked me if I thought they had anything to worry about, being in business with Tupac. I told him absolutely not. I told him the same thing that I told everyone else—that Tupac was a consummate pro.

By the time we did *Gridlock'd*, he was also somebody who had been through a lot of negative stuff. He had been shot in New York. He had been in jail. He had signed with Death Row. By the time we finished *Gridlock'd*, I'm convinced that he had made a change. I think it was a change he had started thinking about while he was incarcerated. I think Death Row and that whole experience . . . I think he saw that as a necessary means to an end. And I'm pretty sure that by the time he was shot in Las Vegas, he had already started to implement the plan to extricate himself from Death Row. He did and said things that made me know he was headed in a new direction.

Michael Kuhn didn't have a clue who Tupac was when we first started talking about casting him in *Gridlock'd*. His boss, Allain Levy, trusted Russell Simmons' judgment when it came to people in the music business, especially because Russell was telling people that this kid was a star. Of course by the time *Gridlock'd* came out, even Michael knew who he was and was finally starting to listen to me about allowing us to make movies with him on an ongoing basis. And that was something Tupac really wanted to do. We managed to get Michael to agree to give Def Pictures money that would be specifically earmarked to develop films with and for Tupac.

I remember one day while we were shooting, Michael decided he wanted to meet Tupac. So I made sure to tell Tupac he was coming and I wanted to introduce them. When I

Tupac with Preston's daughter and her friends.

got to the set Tupac was out in back of his trailer playing basketball with some of the security guards and drivers and whatnot. He had his shirt off and he was sweating and talking shit like he was on the playground. And so I went over to him and told him the guy I mentioned, the head of the studio, was on his way. So Michael got there and got out of his limo, and Tupac stopped playing ball and met him in his trailer. And I was in awe as I watched him win over this guy by just being himself. After we left the trailer, I walked Michael back to his limo and he said, "What an incredible young man."

I have a daughter, Naima, who was about seventeen at the time we were making *Gridlock'd*. She was staying with me for the summer with a girlfriend of hers. And of course Tupac was God to them. They got to hang out with him a little bit. Just before they left to go home to the East Coast, they wanted to see him one more time. I called him up and he said sure. He told me to bring them by the set of a music video he was involved in. Not his, but someone else's.

So that day we were getting ready to go and of course the girls spent hours getting themselves all cute. When they came out of their room to go, I was appalled at what my daughter had on, or what she didn't have on. I was like, "Where the hell are you going dressed like that?" So we got into this big beef about their outfits. Before long, I gave up and we just went. When we arrived, security was all over the place. They radioed up to Pac and he came down and walked up to us and stopped. He said to my daughter and her friend, "Why y'all dressed like that? You are ladies, aren't you? Well, dress like ladies. If you dress like that with these knuckleheads around here, they are gonna think you're something else and they're gonna treat you like that." He made a distinction between a certain kind of girl that is always on those video sets and other women. Period. Not just my daughter.

When we gave Tupac the script for *In Too Deep*, he loved it. It was about a guy going undercover and losing it to the dark side. Kind of like the clinical split-personality thing. We were talking about the movie and I'll never forget it. I said something like, "I can't imagine what it would be like to really be two different people inside the same body." And Tupac looked at me and said, "I can. Because I am."

GEORGE PRYCE

> As Tupac's publicist while he was signed to Death Row Records, George Pryce, aka "Papa G," spent the last nine months of Tupac's life trying to keep Tupac's interviews and appearances organized and the media frenzy at the label contained.

I first met Tupac the night he was released from prison and immediately flown to Los Angeles. The entire staff at Death Row had been instructed to participate in a welcoming dinner for him that night at Monte's Steakhouse in Westwood Village. All the Death Row artists were present for a lavish meal of prime rib, steaks, and lobster—and of course the Louis Roederer Cristal champagne flowed like water.

That night Tupac and I met only briefly, but the complexity of the man showed immediately. His demeanor was strong, but appeared vulnerable and of course weary from the ordeal that he had just been sprung from.

In preparation for his arrival and the announcement of him being signed to Death Row, I had arranged for one-on-one interviews with every major television network, magazine, and newspaper throughout the United States and Europe. The day after the dinner, when I tried to reach him at the Beverly Hills Peninsula Hotel, I was blown away when I was informed that he was already in the studio, working on his premiere album for the label.

Over the next nine months, which seemed more like nine years in my memory, we fought verbally, rejoiced together over good press, cursed and condemned over the bad, we laughed and confided in each other.

LISA LOPES

> The late Lisa Lopes, aka "Left Eye," made up a third of the best-selling girl group of her era, the Grammy Award–winning TLC. The two developed a connection that Lisa always felt would outlast their time.

I first met Tupac at the end of 1991. TLC had just recorded our debut album, but we weren't out yet. We had just released a video and I think that how's he knew about me. And I knew about him 'cause I'd just seen him on a talk show venting about Arsenio Hall. I thought he was a very interesting person. I was very pleased when I met him because he was everything I expected and more.

He was so artistic. He made me a tape with music on it. I'm not talking about his music, but classical, jazz, blues. There were songs that I had never even heard of. It really opened my eyes to where his head was.

Shortly after he released the album with "Brenda's Got a Baby," Tupac started getting letters from women who were in that same situation. I will never forget how he expressed to me that he actually wanted to go out and make a personal visit to each of these women who had written a letter to him. I thought that was pretty special. I believe that every song that he recorded speaks for him. There's not one song that doesn't.

Tupac was a reflection of me. Some of the questions that are unanswered in my mind, I can listen to a Tupac song and the answer will jump right out and hit me in the head. I look at his interviews, I look at the way his life was, I see a lot of me. I was born on May 27 and he was born on June 16. We were two weeks apart.

I got a chance to go to his house a few months before he passed away, and it was a very weird experience because everything I had in my cabinets he had in his cabinets—down to the seasonings in the kitchen, the types of foods that he would eat, the pot set, the chairs that we sat in. It made me wonder, "Wow, have I been cooking for the wrong man all these years?"

Tupac stood for the truth. Being real. He was a tragic hero and a legend in his own right. He represented both sides of the coin. He was from one extreme to the next. There was almost no in-between. He is probably one of the most honest, the most truthful, realest entities that I have ever encountered. He would call it how he saw it. He wouldn't hold back. But he had a very big heart. A very, very big heart. It was to the tenth power.

Painting Lisa created for Tupac in 1992. A letter she wrote on the back says that ten years from then, they'd be together. Lisa died in a car accident in 2002.

SNOOP DOGG

> Hip-hop icon Snoop Dogg has become a household name and an international star. He and Tupac shared a business relationship, but also a friendship that Snoop still treasures to this day.

The first time I met Pac was at the *Poetic Justice* rap party. I introduced myself and he introduced himself to me. I had seen him in the movie *Juice* and I told him how I thought it was dope and how I liked how he got down. He said the same kind of thing back to me, so we rolled a blunt up and smoked a bleavy outside. When we went back inside the party, John Singleton had me get on the microphone. I did a little freestyle and Pac got on, too. After we did that, we exchanged numbers. We just connected. Everything he liked, I liked. We were like brothers.

Right after that, he invited me over to his house and made shrimp and fish for a nigga. He had his apron on and everything. He had that little batter, frying up some shrimp. It was crazy. He was up in that muthafucka doin' it. Rated R and Big Syke were there posted up. I remember he gave me a copy of *Juice* on laser disc so I could watch it again. That's how long ago that was—DVDs weren't even out yet. He had it on laser disc. So I went home that night and popped it in and was like, "Yeah, this nigga's hard."

I remember right after I beat my [court] case, we went down to Mexico. Suge took us down there. We did this shit called parasailing. They put a nigga in the sky. Me and Pac did it together. We were riding around up in the sky together. And when we were up there, he was telling me about this idea for a movie where I die and I come back and I'm a ghost and I'm talking to you. And he was saying, "Yeah, you beat your case nigga." And all of a sudden Suge grabbed the controls from the boat dude and he just dunked us in the middle of the ocean. Literally in the middle of the fuckin' ocean. We were sitting in the ocean with our feet in the water and we were scared than a muthafucka screaming, "Let us up—there could be sharks up in here." Suge was laughing and shit and would bring us halfway up and then put us back down. That was just such a fun moment because that was when we all really loved each other.

I learned a lot from Pac. I learned how to be aggressive in the studio. He put more emphasis on working in the studio and being creative and getting shit done. It was like a food

Snoop and Tupac at the 1996 MTV Video Music Awards.

chain up in there when he was in the studio. He didn't waste any muthafuckin' time. He ain't in there talking any bullshit. He ain't in there on the phone. He's not doing anything but music. And nowadays my spirit is the same way. That's why I'm able to do so many things. And be a chameleon. That's why I'm able to act, and do TV and music. Before I was just content on being the dopest rapper. And that was cool with me. He showed me how to be hungry and attack everything I wanted to do.

We talked like we were two presidents. Like Clinton and Malcolm X. Like on boss shit. Like we're the leaders and our soldiers are our soldiers. And if we have a problem with each other we stay within the structure of being organized and being military-minded. He was strategic about all his moves, being in the studio, how we need to conduct ourselves. How we need to act. Everything. So a lot of the things that happened were very well planned out. And even though I was a leader, leading the Dogg Pound, I accepted my role as a student. When Pac came, I allowed him to become a part of the leadership of Death Row.

He was real loving. I remember there was a time that my wife and I weren't seeing eye-to-eye on anything. We were going through a lot back then. I talked a lot about being on my own. Everyone from Death Row was like, "Yeah, the bitches love you Snoop, you need to be by yourself." But Tupac was like, "Fuck what these niggas is talking about. You need to go home and be with your girl and your baby. That's where you need to be." And he helped me stick it out with my wife. That always stayed in the back of my head, that he'd seen something special in me and my girl.

Later in our careers, when he got out of prison, I was living in a condo on Wilshire and he came over and was like, "I gotta get me one of these." I think I was on the fourth floor and he was on the sixth floor. He had a Rolls-Royce. I had a Rolls-Royce. We dressed the same. We wore suits. We were high fashion. We weren't on no rap nigga with a gold chain and five dollars in our pocket shit. We were on some boss shit 'cause we had these big adventurous dreams in mind. Certain movies inspired us. We really felt like we could fall off into those roles in real life.

Tupac would always be on my side during my court case. He'd show up to court with a suit on, representing. It was that genuine love. He was the type of individual where if he loves you, he loves the shit out of you—but if he hates you, he hates the fuck out of you. There was no in-between. He was a cool dude with a sweet personality, not on nothing soft, but on some real man shit as far being sentimental enough to understand certain things in life. Like the whole thing when he convinced me to stay with my wife and my son—he didn't have no kids or one particular woman but he still understood that meant more than anything to me, more than any record we made, any chicks we may have got at, videos we did, or trips we took.

His legacy is so fucking big, there's people in Haiti, there's people in Africa, there's people in Japan, all over the whole world who idolize him, who have immortalized him. His legacy is bigger than anybody can imagine. People liked him when he was alive. But they loved him when he was dead. I saw how muthafuckas flipped it when he died and started loving him as opposed to loving him when he was walking this earth, because he was so controversial, so ahead of his time. He was so creative that a lot of his messages sped right past you. But I loved that nigga from the start.

His body is gone. But his spirit will never die.

If I could talk to Tupac today, I'd love to see where his growth would be now as a person. He was so hot-tempered and spontaneous. I toned it down and became a grown man. Now, I put out more fires than starting them. I put more water on fires now than gasoline. And I would have loved to have seen his growth and development.

My oldest son was like one or two years old when he met Tupac. My sons love Tupac. My youngest son never got to meet him. They love his music. My son is sayin' shit and cussing and everything, and I let him do it when he listens to Tupac. I'm his favorite rapper, but Tupac is the shit I hear the most around the house.

STEP JOHNSON

> Step Johnson has been a major player in the music industry since the 1970s. As the president of Urban Music at Interscope Geffen A&M, he works with artists like 50 Cent, Eminem, Mary J. Blige, and Snoop Dogg.

I had just come from Capitol to Interscope when I met Tupac. And back then there were only three people in the whole urban department. John McClean brought me over. I met Tupac many times. The first meeting with him was at the old Interscope building. He looked like a little boy. He was real nice, very respectful. He was dedicated to his music. His music was his life. His music was his drug. His music was his energy. You could see it. If you talked to him for a minute, you would realize he was much older than what he actually was.

People always ask me, "What do you know about Pac?" My introduction to Tupac was through [Tom] Whalley. Whalley told me he was one-of-a-kind, that he was unbelievable. I didn't know the Pac that most people knew. I didn't know that guy. He was always respectful. I never heard him curse or get nasty. When he was around me, he was always a gentleman.

I'll never forget the first time I saw Pac perform. We were in Atlanta. The place was just packed. He was rockin' the stage. There had to be about twenty other dudes up there with him, but you knew who Tupac was. Shirt off. Doin' his thing. Actin' a fool. Carryin' on.

I have never seen anybody else who knew where his or her life was going. Who knew what life meant. I will go to my grave saying that this kid had a premonition . . . that he knew. He was so dedicated to his music, Pac could stay in the studio 24/7 for six months and never think about coming out. He knew things that the average person didn't know. There is a thin line between insanity and genius, and he walked that line very closely. Because at any minute he was a genius like you wouldn't believe. And any minute he could be totally, totally nuts. So you really had to know him.

I had two different lives with Tupac. I knew him before Death Row and during Death Row. I saw the changes in his life. He was always the same person but walking that thin line. You don't threaten him. You don't challenge him. You don't sell him a wolf ticket 'cause he will buy it. I don't care who you are, how big you are, I don't care if you're the police. If you come at him and challenge him, 6'5", 300 pounds, or 5'2", 85 pounds, if you challenge him, he's gonna take the challenge. That's just the way he was.

He had a lot of love in his heart. He loved his people.

Tupac knew the difference between a black man and a nigga. Like he said, some of us were niggas. And a lot of us, a majority of us, were black people trying to survive and trying to make it. He understood that. If you listen to his music, he is one of the few artists who tells stories. He really was a modern-day storyteller. If we were in Africa back in the day, he'd be one of the elders who would talk to kids about their lives and what was going on. At the same time, if you pushed him, he would be one of the first warriors to pick up a sword or a spear to go get your ass. He had no fear of death.

What Elvis is to pop, and Bob Marley is to reggae, Tupac is to hip-hop. Fifty years from now we will still be hearing about Elvis. We will still be hearing about Bob Marley. And we will still be hearing about Tupac. You may not like him, but you will learn from him.

I've been in this business over twenty-five years and I've met a lot of people. There are very few people that I think I was fortunate to meet in the entertainment industry. And he would probably have to be one of the most impressionable, one of the most talented. I just wish people would've known the other side of him—not the stuff they saw in Las Vegas and not the stuff they saw in New York. I wish they really knew him.

I always say there is a reason why the federal government, the police departments, why a lot of authority-type agencies took a look after this kid. They don't take a look after you if you're a fool or if you don't got nothing to say. So why would they take a look at him? All these rappers out here today and your major concern was Pac? Let's think about that.

We need more heroes. It doesn't mean riding in here with the white horse with the white hat. Our kids don't know who that is. Our kids need to know what Tupac was about. That he wasn't this thug. That he wasn't this gangster. And if you understand what he meant by Thug Life you would understand what he is about. People have a tendency to take those words and twist them into what they want you to believe. He had a message. He delivered his message. And it's up to us to go and see and listen and continue that message. We need to let him be known for who he truly is.

We should never ever, ever forget this kid. Ever.

QD3

> QD3, a record producer and the son of the legendary Quincy Jones, had a close personal and professional relationship with Tupac.

Once I found out that a friend of mine and Tupac had connected, I wanted to send him some beats, so she gave me the address to where he was at. So I slipped a tape under his hotel door. He called back the same night. He said, "Yeah, I liked all of them, let's go do it. These are exactly the type of tracks I was looking for to finish up the album."

Tupac had a thing about time—you *had* to show up on time. He had told me to be at the studio at 7 p.m., but it was raining. I got there about a half an hour late and he kind of looked at me sideways and said, "Hey, you're late."

The very first impression I had, I came in the room and all the Outlawz, Snoop, and Dre were there. Pac was running around, smoking, and rapping one of his songs. I remember how powerful that image was—Tupac doing his thing, with the bullet holes and all that shit. It was crazy, but it was a very positive first impression.

Working with him in the studio was incredible. I think in your heart, you would love for an artist just to come in and take control of their vision without any second guessing, but I had never seen that before. Before I worked with Tupac, I was one of those people who would sit there forever and tweak stuff. Pac slapped that out of me quick. No tweaking or anything. "Just do it" kind of shit. "You can do all that stuff when I'm gone," he said. It was amazing, working with somebody who brings 200 percent to your track, and that fast, and with no thought. Just the energy that he had was inspiring. I've never worked the same since, it's more intuitive now.

Everybody else in the business did songs piece-by-piece. They asked for a lot of opinions, and there was a long process of discussing what's right for the record and all that kind of crap, whereas with Pac there wasn't any of that. He just went in and did it and left.

Once we were in the studio, everybody was drinking, smoking, having fun type of shit, including him. He was telling everyone a story, and writing something at the same time. He handed me some sheets of paper after about fifteen or twenty minutes of this, and it was a treatment for his video. With exterior, interior shots, angles, the whole nine, and he'd done that while he was talking, didn't even make a big deal out of it. That's how he would write his lyrics, too. He would just sit there and talk to you, smoking his weed and cracking jokes. All of a sudden, he'd say, "All right, let's go," and then he'd run in the recording booth, and you wouldn't even know what the song was about.

All that added up to him being better in person than anything you could imagine, which is the opposite of what normally happens. That's where he had that black Jesus vibe, because when you were around him, you'd feel like you could do anything. He was so driven and he didn't have that "Well, what if we do X . . . what if Y happens?" None of that. It was like, "Thug, we gotta run and get to point B."

He had a lot of fun, but the vibe could change quickly. Everything everybody says about that is true . . . . One minute he'd be laughing and cracking jokes. Then he'd change. One night when we were working and having fun, Nate Dogg came in and was like, "Yo, our trailer just got shot up in New York." And Pac, he went off like it was *his* problem. He wanted to take every battle on. There was honor behind it, but I felt like he was an inch away from maturing out of the fight stance.

At the end of his life, I think he'd found who he wanted to be and he was working toward it. Basically, he wanted to be a more mature person who could execute on all the great ideas he had. I think he was almost there, but I also got a really manic feeling from him. Like *real* manic in the studio. I'd give him a ballad and he would yell at the top of his lungs on it. But that's part of what made him great.

STILL
LISTENING

"Tupac was skydiving without a parachute. It was almost like he knew his purpose and wasn't fighting. And he settled into that purpose. He more or less fulfilled his prophecy. If you look at him in the car that night he got shot, he had that look on his face, a look of concern and despair. He had some issues with happiness, too. Pac had a lot of pain as well as a lot of joy. That's why you had a lot of pain in those records. It was his therapy. And his lyrics were also medicine for his listeners. So when he died it was like, okay, I felt like he could breathe. For the first time, he can breathe. No more expectations, no more pain. You can breathe now."

—L.T. Hutton

"Tupac is the largest-selling rap artist. I think it's because of his consistency and work ethic. There are still new albums that haven't been fully released. There's new music to come. It's not over yet. He's our Elvis."

—50 Cent

"The world lost a leader when Tupac died. We don't know what he would've gone on to. If Oprah Winfrey had only lived until she was twenty-five, we would have lost a relatively unknown, local-market TV anchorwoman. If Malcolm X died at twenty-five, we would have lost a hustler named Detroit Red."

—Quincy Jones

NAS

> Though the out-of-control East Coast–West Coast rivalry in the hip-hop world led to a heated battle of hearsay between Tupac and Nas, the two rappers settled their differences just days before Tupac was murdered.

The first time I heard Tupac, he was in Digital Underground doin' "Same Song." I was used to the members in the Digital Underground group, but when Pac came on I was like, "Oh, okay, they got a more serious rapper in the camp—someone to look forward to hearing from." What immediately got me was that he was rockin' the African shit in the video.

I met him after the movie *Juice* came out. We were on the Howard University college campus, during the time when everyone used to drive down there and just kick it for Homecoming. You'd bump into everybody—rappers, athletes, actors, drug dealers. I saw Tupac talking to some girls, and I handed him a Hennessy bottle. I probably shouldn't have had it with me, because I was on campus, but he took it and turned it bottom up. He kept reciting one of my rhymes off my first single over and over again—a song called "Halftime." "When it's my time to go, I'll wait for God." He loved that line.

Later on during our careers, Tupac started having his drama with Bad Boy. Then other people started getting affiliated with it. Then he went for Mobb Deep. After that, there was no one else to go after but me. So it was like, any day now he's gonna say my name. But he never said it. The tension was so high that rumors started. Rumors like, "Tupac dissed you, Tupac dissed you." I heard he dissed me at House of Blues over the Friends Whodini beat that we used for "If I Ruled the World." After I heard he did that, I was in Atlanta doing a show, and I went on the microphone and said, "Fuck Tupac." Automatically, there was this underground tension, this buzzing and people talking. But I didn't hear my name on any of his records, I never recorded his name, either. When he put my name on *Makaveli*, it was so far gone by then that it was beef time.

At the MTV Awards, I saw Tupac when I was coming through the backstage before he was about to present an award. I said, "What's up, brotha?" And he said, "What's up, brotha?" It was really sarcastic. A few of my guys had bumped into a few of his guys, and had some words in the lobby of the place. Then we all ended up at Bryant Park for an after-party.

He came to the park with about fifty niggas. And I had fifty niggas with me. We both stood there in the middle of the park, and I saw him and called him. He took a breath and walked right to me and we started talking. The first thing I say is, "I heard you're dissin' me on your new album." I thought he was gonna say, "Naw, that's all rumors, like everything else." But he's like, "Yeah. I heard the mix tapes on your new album and it seems like you throwin' the shit my way, and people are telling me that you're coming at me, so I had to get prepared and I did what I had to do."

Then he said, "Me and you, we brothers. Me and you, we aren't supposed to ever go at it. Why we went at it? My shit was with Mobb Deep. My shit was with Biggie. Why did you get into it?"

I said, "You can't go at Mobb Deep 'cause those are my niggas."

We both had so many niggas there, and there started to be all this tension. The news cameras started coming around, and it started getting rowdy, so we knew we had to take it to another place later. But he said he would try to make the changes, to take my name off the *Makaveli* album, and he was also talking about bringing everybody together to do something with niggas from all over. He wanted to bring the shit together. He talked about maybe meeting in Vegas the weekend of the Tyson fight so we could keep talking, 'cause he believed that we were the two to bring it all together.

I was so excited that he said that, 'cause I felt like in a way we were kindred spirits. When he said that, I knew he felt the same way, and after that I was totally cool. The beef was never supposed to have happened between us.

He was known by his birth name, Tupac. Tupac. Nas. Nasir's my birth name. So when you're talking about artists like us, we're bearing our souls, no matter what backlash, or who comes to kill us, we're bearing our souls, because it's *my* name. It's *me* you're buying. You're not buying MC this. You're buying Nas. You're buying Tupac. We were named these names from the dark continent. It's some ancestor shit. I saw him as that. Without being strange and weird and shit, we both knew each other before this shit. Period.

Tupac was a community person, and if he were still here, he'd have inspired me to become more active. He would have made me brave by just watching him. I think Martin and Malcolm motivated each other. I think different people are able to motivate each other to perform better and to get things done. He was going to be a black leader. He already was a leader, but he was going to make that shit official. And he would've shown our whole generation how that's done. 'Cause we didn't see it. We didn't see Martin Luther King catch them blows to the head. We didn't see Eazy-E revolutionize the game so that now muthafuckas can make millions of dollars off rap. We only benefit from these muthafuckas, and then we forget their struggle. We forget there was a Malcolm that really put his life on the line for us. So when we don't see Tupac around, we don't have people who are motivated because they don't understand what his plight was. So I needed him here to remind me. But I'm all right . . . I got it.

> Nas appeared on both the record and in the video of the single "Thugz Mansion," a posthumous Tupac release. The video was nominated for an MTV Video Music Award for Best Rap video in 2003.

COMMON

> Though rap artist Common and Tupac only crossed paths once, Tupac left a strong impression that affected Common throughout his career.

Tupac influenced me in a lot of ways. When I met him, he treated me with a lot of love. It was like, he dug what I did, or at least that's what I felt. I got to perform with him one time in Chicago. The police and security guards were out of control and he stood up for me and my crew and I stood up for his and we were just talking shit to the security guards.

"Dear Mama" was one of Tupac's songs that influenced me the most; it was one of the most heartfelt songs I've ever heard in hip-hop. It also showed that you could be a real cat but still express compassionate love. You could be talking about the street but still talking about how everybody loved their mama. The song was bigger than any other song—not just bigger by record sales, but bigger sounding. I had never heard nobody doing nothing like this. The music sounded beautiful. It showed courage. And I couldn't believe he came out with another song again right after. That was the first time I noticed a hip-hop artist doing an album, and then having a whole new song that soon.

All people need to see that drive he had. Children need to see it, and know that it's important that you believe in yourself. It's important that you acknowledge that although you may be messed up over here, you know where you're striving to be. It's important that you be a warrior. It's important that you embrace your people. Tupac's legacy was all that, and it's very important that we pass it on to the youth. His is one of the most important legacies of our time. That's why it's still alive. Nobody, no rapper, will have the impact on this time and space like Tupac had, so we better cherish his legacy and absorb everything we learned from it.

The body may deteriorate, but Tupac is still alive in a way by his spirit being here. We will always talk about Tupac the way we talk about Marvin Gaye and Bob Marley.

LEILA STEINBERG

> Soon after Tupac relocated to Marin City, he met Leila Steinberg. Leila was not only a fellow poet, but also a friend, a confidante, and Tupac's very first manager.

Pac's voice was—and still is—international. He was part of a movement, separate from the artist, he was really consciously a political voice. We had serious plans. He understood that he was a political vehicle and a political voice because of his birthright. He believed his art was his tool.

Years after Pac died, I went to Soweto, South Africa, on his birthday, June 16, because that's where Pac and I always talked about going, because of the racial strife and hardship that we wanted to change. The 1976 massacre in Soweto marked what would become the turning point for ending apartheid. What was once a tragic day was now a celebrated date because of what was accomplished through all the loss and sacrifice. What's more, it was also June 16.

I was on the bus, and a young woman, her name was Dimpo, asked me what I was doing there. I told her that I had a friend from the States who was a rap artist. I told her he'd died, that his birthday is June 16, and that he'd always wanted to go to Soweto. When I told her that I was speaking about Tupac Shakur, she said she couldn't believe it. She told me that her friends and family hold Tupac in the highest regard. That the love they have for Tupac parallels their love for Mandela. Wow, if Tupac could've heard what she was saying, it would have touched him so deeply. I can still hear his laugh so vividly, I can picture him with his bright, wide eyes, saying, "Did you hear that shit, Leila? She just compared me to Mandela!"

Dimpo wanted to take me somewhere. She told me that when I understood how important Tupac is to her family and all of the people in Soweto, I would know why our trip was necessary.

We got off the bus at the main square, where there was a memorial exhibit for the Soweto massacre. There was this huge display of life-sized pictures, graphic pictures of kids who'd been killed in it. Poetry was written all over it. It was really heavy, you could just feel the energy in the square.

Dimpo still wanted me to walk somewhere with her. I was five months pregnant, walking through this township with both of my young daughters, Talia and Devanee, not

A quiet moment between Tupac and Leila at a Mac Mall video shoot.

knowing where I was going. She was determined to show me something. So after a long walk, we stood in front of what looked like an old wooden cottage. It was the township's phone bank, where everyone went to make phone calls if they needed to. Dimpo was so excited she was covering my eyes and guiding my footsteps. She wanted me to walk into the building without seeing. God knows why but there I was, stepping into the unknown. I was standing in the center of the room when she uncovered my eyes. To my utter amazement, the entire room was one big Tupac shrine. I mean literally. From the candles burning all over the dimly lit room to blown-up copies of his poetry, to notes and poems on the walls written by the kids.

I was blown away.

CHRIS HAYES

> Chris Hayes is a Green Bay Packers Super Bowl champion to some, but he's a mentor to many, reaching out to the community through his non-profit organization, 30-30 Hayes.

My walk in life was different than Tupac's. He was gifted in the entertainment realm and I was gifted with athletic ability. But still I could relate to his music because we both came from the neighborhood. Just like anybody else that comes from the same type of upbringing. We all can relate. We all come from the same place. Having to survive and do whatever it takes.

The industries of music and sports go hand-in-hand. It's just the struggle that brings us all together. You got sports figures who always want to be rappers and you have rappers who always want to be sports cats. The reason for this is because most of us come from the base of the neighborhood. Just being African American and being from the hood, you know, you had to find things to do. You was beating on trash cans as drums. You had to figure it out yourself. It all becomes so much a part of who you are. I tell people all the time, I'm a product of my neighborhood and I'm proud of it.

During the whole East Coast–West Coast thing I was playing for the Jets. I used to go speak in the detention centers out there. The issues coming from the kids were all Tupac and Biggie. They'd really identify you with Tupac or Biggie Smalls, like, "Are you West Coast?," and, "Oh, that's a Tupac nigga." Biggie and Tupac turned it upside down for a while.

The month Tupac was killed, I was playing for the Green Bay Packers. We were just starting the season that we ended up winning the Super Bowl in. I remember seeing the news report about him getting laid back on the strip in Vegas. But I was like, "That's Tupac, he'll be all right." That week in the locker room everybody was saying, "Naw, Tupac ain't gonna die." Nobody thought he was gonna die.

I think Tupac was a victim of the streets. A victim of circumstance. I believe he was killed for what he represented and what he believed in. I think there were numerous events that led up to his death. I think that who he was and the force he potentially had is why he is not breathing today. I wish it wouldn't have happened like that because that brotha, if he was still here, could've impacted people's lives on a whole different level. And it's Tupac's music that captured everything that people were going through and wanted to say. There's no one here now to do that in the way that he did.

NIKKI GIOVANNI

> Touched by both Tupac's life and his death, poet Nikki Giovanni wrote the poem "All Eyez on You," which was published in her 1997 collection, *Love Poems.* She also decided to honor Tupac by getting "Thug Life" tattooed on her arm.

I first heard of Tupac when my son, Tommy, came home one day and said, "Mommy, do you know Tupac?" I told him I didn't. He told me about Digital Underground, and how they gave me a shout-out. And when I learned that the Tupac he spoke about was Tupac *Shakur*, I immediately made the connection that Tupac was Afeni Shakur's son.

All of us—my whole generation—were aware of who Afeni was during the time she was pregnant. Pac was about three years younger than my son. All of us wished them well when Tupac was born. I know I did. And then to see him making his way in the arts, I thought it was great—it was a good thing to see someone coming out of so much strife. There's a lot of unhappiness in the world, and Tupac and Afeni had a difficult life. His mother was a believer; she was a Panther. You knew that because of his mother, Tupac would be a very solid man, and that you could lean on him.

I wrote the poem "All Eyez on You" that Saturday he died, because when you're sad, the only thing you can do is write. It was just incredibly sad. You just get tired of it. Every time someone great comes along, somebody shoots them. And still I needed to figure out something to do to honor his spirit. I remembered his tattoo and I thought I'd drive from Blacksburg to Roanoke to a place called Alex's Tattoo, 'cause I'd heard it was a really good place. I said to the guy there, "I wanna get a tattoo." And he said, "Well, go and look at the ones on the wall and see what you want." I said, "No, I have a special one in mind. I want it to say 'Thug Life.'" He said, "You don't look like a thug." And I said, "Yeah, I'm a thug. I'm with the thugs out there."

When I share that with my students, they all just scream because they all love him. I mean, when you look at the spoken word and the number of young people who are rapping and having throw downs, all of that is coming from Tupac. They love him. He means as much to them as James Dean meant to his generation. I'm an old jazz fan. Nobody thinks about Louis Armstrong as being dead because we see his influence. You can't talk about jazz music unless you talk about Louis. And I think with Tupac, it's the same thing. Tupac is an icon.

Nikki showing her **Thug Life** tattoo.

I think if Tupac were still here, he'd be involved in politics. I don't think he was crazy, so I don't think he'd actually run for office, but I think he'd lend support—the same way Puffy does "Vote or Die." All of that community and political activism comes from Pac. I don't think he would be with the neo-con Negros; I think he would have been with the progressives. The trajectory was very clear.

I so appreciate what Afeni has been doing, by keeping Tupac's legacy alive. Because losing a child has got to be the worst thing in the world that could happen to anybody. Every time she reads something he wrote, or hears his voice, it just has to tear at her heart. But she's being strong, because it's what you have to do. I so admire her for that. And having lost his physical self, she continues to keep his cultural self alive. I think that's so important; so often in the black community we lose people, because we have no ability to keep what they were doing out there. Like what they are doing to King for example. You would think that Martin just woke up one morning and said to Coretta, I have a dream. But it was much more than that. There were serious things done.

Afeni is keeping *all* parts of Tupac's image alive. I think it's essential. She's very lucky in that Tupac was such a great artist, he was charismatic, and he looked good. So she's able to keep it going. The young kids still want him. I'm talking to kids now who have actually never seen him, but they have a sense of his power and a sense of his heart. They love him like they knew him, like they woke up this morning and said, "Hey, Pac, how you doin'?" And Pac said, "I'm doing fine."

BARON DAVIS

> Even though All-Star NBA player Baron Davis never had the chance to meet him, Tupac's life and work left a lasting impression on Baron and many of his NBA teammates. Even now, Tupac's music plays a key role in Baron's pre-game rituals.

I liked Tupac so much that when I first started in the league I went by the alias "Tupac" and when we traveled, I used to get my rooms under his name. When I went to different cities, my friends and family would know to call the hotel and ask for "Tupac." I gotta hear "Hail Mary" on my way to play a game, to get pumped up, and then I usually rap "So Many Tears" right before the game. I really live and die by him.

Being a young black male raised in the inner city, and being that I went to a private arts and sciences school called Crossroads, I used to study Tupac's story, even when he was still alive. We had very similar backgrounds. He was someone who was willing to understand where we are as a community as blacks and as whites. I was raised on his music and in kind of the same environment. I can understand what goes on in the ghetto. I also try to do what I can to help people see the future and where we need to be and where we need to grow to. So a lot of Tupac lives in me.

And his music lives on. He lives in a lot of basketball players and entertainers who are trying to do the right thing, especially the younger guys. I think every athlete who listens to his music feels the same way about him. To most people who come from impoverished neighborhoods, he's a hero. He's a martyr.

CYNTHIA MCKINNEY

> Cynthia McKinney served twelve years in the House of Representatives, and was the first African-American woman to represent the state of Georgia. A great Tupac supporter, she can be heard quoting his lyrics on the steps of the United States Capitol in her documentary, *American Blackout.*

Tupac has affected my life in two key areas. One, because I'm a mother; and two, because I held a public position that allowed me to transmit some of my thoughts about his impact.

When my son was going through his teenage years, it was very difficult for me to engage in a conversation with him. I would try to talk to him about his day at school, his friends, his teachers, his world. I wanted to know what was going on in that head of his and if I, as a mother, had fulfilled my responsibilities to transmit certain values to him. But my son was, at that time, extremely quiet. I would ask him a question and would basically get a grunt for an answer. At most I would get one word. "Yeah." "Fine." My son was an expert at giving a one-word response to any question that I posed. But there was one strategy I employed to communicate more effectively, and that was to listen to his music. 'Cause he was all into music. And when I asked him who his favorite singer was, his response was, "Tupac."

So I set out to know who Tupac was. I went online and got his lyrics. They were so potent. There was so much power in them. I remember one song, "Changes." I was up all night playing that song and going line by line through the music on the CD, to try and figure out the words he was saying. And every line was as important as the previous line, and more important, and the content was so technical and so political and so insightful that I couldn't stop, I literally could not put it down, this project of deciphering the lyrics of "Changes." Then from "Changes" I went to "Brenda's Got a Baby" and then through the rest of his collection.

My son is a first generation iPod kid. But he didn't download any free Tupac CDs. He *bought* those, because it was a powerful message that you wanted to contribute to; the mission of this messenger was so important that it was important to put your dollars behind the purchase of the CD. My son was very proud of the fact that he bought every Tupac CD. And I listened to them all, and became a devotee of Tupac myself. There are the party songs, and there are songs about what young vibrant men are supposed to be. But then there is this child who possesses an incredible insight into the very being, the heart of the United States of America, who comes from a family that is dedicated to making America live up to its noblest ideal for every American. As a mother, I have to say one of my favorite songs is "Dear Mama." I also love "Dear Mr. President." He's petitioning his government because the conditions are horrible. He's telling him, "You said you were gonna do something about it—well DO SOMETHING ABOUT IT, MR. PRESIDENT!"

After Tupac died, I was approached by C. Delores Tucker and invited to participate in one of the press conferences she had that attacked hip-hop. Tucker had been a supporter of mine when I needed it, from the very first day I was sworn into Congress. The idea of America being the place that it is supposed to be for all Americans has been my mission— and something that has not been lost on my son. So it was amazing that I would get pushed into the hip-hop world by my son, and at the same time my political friend C. Delores Tucker was pushing in another direction.

I chose not to participate in Tucker's press conference, and eventually explained why I did not in a series of speeches, and my explanation went something like this: "My son is a hip-hopper. My son loves hip-hop music. And if I see something wrong with a culture that my son embraces, then rather than push my son away, I will embrace that culture and try to instill my values so that my values are reflected in it." I felt compelled to make a public statement because I had traveled all over the country under C. Delores Tucker's embrace, but I couldn't go the next step.

I'm sitting here at my kitchen table and it's just a matter of coincidence that I have *Pac's Life* sitting here. My son doesn't even know I got it, 'cause he's away at school. But I bought it and I love the CD. And let me tell you what I did: I took it to the next generation. I went to my mother who has the "oh, those children—I don't understand the baggy pants" attitude. And I started talking to her about my revelations about Tupac and I took her to see *Resurrection*. And now my mother, who is seventy-something years old, now she's a Tupac fan. Now she fully understands Tupac's message and where he came from. I am so happy to have been able to find a way to express my interest in hip-hop culture, and support young people who create that culture.

MIKE EPPS

> Mike Epps proudly remembers that he would listen to Tupac's music for inspiration as he traveled on the New York City subways, going from comedy club to comedy club on his own journey to Hollywood.

I'm originally from Indiana. I had a rough background. I was sent to some facilities as a youth. I had been shot at, spent time in the penitentiary, was on welfare, had six brothers and one sister, didn't graduate from high school, grew up in the ghetto, didn't have nothing at all at the time I first heard Tupac's music. It was my little brother, who is almost exactly Tupac's age, who turned me on to him. But my little brother was like, "You wanna hear some gangster shit and some real, true shit? Some shit that's all that and pro-black?" I heard it and loved it ever since.

As I became a grown man, I started listening to this man's music and he influenced me to handle things in my life differently. By me being from Indiana, my horizons really weren't broad like they should've been. But his music helped me. He would say some things that I would apply to my life, and it would work. People would be like "Man, how did you do that?" and it was like my little secret. The words were always the same, but he didn't touch everybody like he touched certain people. His music made me feel proud about being black. I just wish I could've met that man and shown him how much I appreciated his lyrics and his activism.

I remember his album *Me Against the World* was one of the albums I used to listen to on the way to the comedy clubs. I would say, "I"m gonna rock this shit. I'm gonna rock the show." I would listen to rap music from the time I left the apartment, got on a train, rode to Brooklyn, got on another train, rode back to Manhattan, to Queens. I had all these tape cassettes of all this different music and I had one with nothing but his music on it. He inspired the shit out of me. Not to the point where I shaved all my hair bald, where I was acting like him. I didn't have a million tattoos. I didn't try to look like him. I am still me.

I always had this passion to talk to kids and try to steer them the right way, because I've had this great luck in my life that allowed me to get into the entertainment industry and change my life. I met this woman named Leila Steinberg, who had known Tupac. She had started a program where she would go into the youth facilities, talking and helping these young children who were at risk, who were criminals coming up and going through all the different departments of corrections. I told Leila that was right up my alley, being that Tupac's music inspired me as a young black man and taught me some things that I didn't even learn from my parents.

For the past three years Leila has been taking me down to Central, right here in Los Angeles, to talk to the kids. We've been going to the Y.A.'s [Youth Authorities]. We've also gone to San Quentin. She mentions that this is a program that Tupac had in mind and that he was going to put forth, and then introduces me as someone—not in the place of Tupac— but like I was one of his employees. So I get up there and introduce myself to the kids and tell them what I've been through. And I am a perfect example, as was Tupac, of how you can change.

I think through his spirit and through his message, he has used me a lot. I think he's used a lot of people who really took what he taught and dedicated themselves to teaching others. I think his spirit runs through those who are committed to that. It's important that we show them a different way and tell them that even with all their hardships and the things that they went through as children, that they still can rise above and be somebody.

EMINEM

> Marshall Mathers, aka Eminem, used to study Tupac's music before he himself became one of the biggest-selling rap artists of all time. In 2004, Eminem was executive producer on Tupac's eighth posthumous album, *Loyal to the Game*.

It's obvious that Tupac has inspired me quite a bit—from his first record to everything since. I mean, if you go back and listen to old material, and then you think this cat was writing this stuff back then. . . . He was so ahead of his time.

In the early days, I used to listen to everyone's different styles. Tupac was putting emotion in his raps, but he was putting compound syllables in there also, and I don't think the average listener was hearing that. I was listening for Big Daddy Kane to hit me off with the "Shake and Brake" and "Make and Take." And I was listening to Run DMC, "once again my friend, not a trend for then, they said rap was crap" and then he'd do the inside rap and come back with the last word rhyming with "friend." I became a student of hip-hop. I listened to everything, but there's not too many people that really struck me more than Tupac did—his persona, his whole everything.

I used to wait for Tupac's videos on *Yo MTV Raps*. The first one I ever saw of Tupac's was "Trapped." And then when I saw "Brenda's Got a Baby" I saw two different sides of this guy. First you saw the thuggish side and then you saw the socially conscious side. I was looking for Tupac interviews after that. Because the way he spoke was so encouraging. He definitely wasn't a prejudiced person, but he stood up for his people. It wasn't like he didn't care about anybody else. He had a message. A lot of people say to me, "how can you go and say this on one record and then go and say this on another record?" Well, it's just that we're not all one-dimensional. Tupac had many dimensions to him. As each album came out you got to see him more in-depth. I think *Me Against the World* was his landmark of finding his sound and finding who he wanted to be, that combination where you could feel compassion for him, but where he didn't back down.

There wasn't much of an age difference between Tupac and me. I felt like I grew up with him. When he came out I felt attached to somebody who basically came from nothing and caught case after case. That's one of the things that unfortunately this man had to go through. I followed just about every situation he got into. I'd hear about little fights at clubs and what I was watching was what seemed like a man torn between fame and keeping that I'm-a-thug image, but also staying humble. He struggled back and forth with that. You could see it in his eyes. He wasn't ready for this kind of stardom.

When "Dear Mama" came out, that song made me wish that I had that kind of relationship with my mother. My mother and I, our relationship was so turbulent and I didn't have a father, so that song really made me wish I had a relationship like that. He taught me to make songs with emotion in them. "Brenda's Got a Baby" put feeling into rap. He captured something that everybody could relate to. If you were poor and you were the underdog, you could relate to what he was saying.

I will never forget, I was nineteen, and my Uncle Ronnie had committed suicide, and it took me a long time to cope with it. The first song I wrote that had any emotion in it like that was called "Troublemaker." It was about my Uncle Ronnie always being looked at as a troublemaker and how nobody ever paid attention to him and how everybody was ignoring him and how he was sending signs that this was going to happen and finally it did. It almost seemed like he was trying to warn people. Part of Tupac's inspiration was him making me not afraid to put emotion into the song, even if the song as I'm writing it is making me teary-eyed as I'm writing it.

There are so many things I can relate to with Tupac. Like him, I moved around and bounced back and forth a lot when I was young. I always used to wonder what it would be like if I got a record deal. When *Me Against the World* came out, he inspired me to just go left and to just not care about what people thought. He taught me to realize that I can't change who I am or the way I was born, what color I am, none of us can. He taught me to be me and to not give a fuck about what people thought about me. Either accept me or don't.

My little girls always ask me about Tupac. They ask what my infatuation with him is about. And why there are so many pictures of him all over the place. They didn't understand it, so I had to explain Tupac to them and they got interested in it. I tell them the story of how he was raised, and how his mother was a Black Panther, and how she was pregnant with him when she was in jail. The story itself is just remarkable.

After I listened to the *Makaveli* album, I didn't have a record deal yet, but that album inspired me to take what I had and use it against myself. If this is what you think of me, I'm gonna say it. As you're thinking about it, I'm gonna say it. And I got into that mode of whatever you're thinking, I'm thinking it, too. I am white. I'm this, I'm that, I'm white trash, think what you wanna think of me, I don't care. So his records would amp me up and that's when I thought of Slim Shady. Who was this person who was really inside me

Dear Afeni,

Sorry if it looks a little sloppy, I could've done a little better if I had the right pencils. Instead, I had to draw it in pen. Plus, I just kind of thought of the idea a little too late. But I've been drawing since I was 10, and I thought you might like it. Anyways, thank you for always being so kind to me. You are a true Queen, and I mean that in every sense of the word. I will never forget the opportunities you have given me. You will always be in my heart, my thoughts, and my prayers. As I have said before, you have no idea how much your son and his music has inspired, not only the "Hip Hop" world, but, speaking for myself, has inspired my whole career. He was, and still is, the true definition of a "Soldier." When I was feeling at my worst; (before fame, before Dre.) I knew I could put that "Tupac" tape in, and suddenly, things weren't so bad. He gave me the courage to stand up and say "F**k the world!" "This is who I am! And if you don't like it, go f**k yourself!" Thank you for giving us his spirit, and yours! God Bless you!

love,
Marshall

A thank-you letter and sketch from Eminem, on display at the Tupac Amaru Shakur Center for the Arts.

To: Afeni - Your friend 4-ever!
-Marshall

and kind of scared to break out of that shell? I look back now and I can see the influence he had on me.

When Tupac got shot, I was at a bar and grill flipping burgers. It just so happens that I was with two members of D12, Kon Artis and Kuniva. They had this big screen TV. I remember Kuniva running into the kitchen during dinner hour when food orders were crazy and he yells, "Yo, someone shot Tupac. Someone shot Tupac." I left all the food laying there and went to the TV. And we're getting yelled at, "Get back to work! What are you doing?" No one understood how serious this was except us. The day we found out he didn't make it we were at the sports bar again, and when we heard, we literally cried. We went into the cleaning closet and Kon Artis said a prayer and we all just hugged and shed a couple tears. We couldn't believe it.

"Life Goes On" is a song that always makes me cry. And that part in "Unconditional Love" when he says "My broken down TV, show cartoons in my living room (hey). One day I hope to make it. A player in this game"—he was connecting with me right there. Even after I got a deal, every Tupac CD ever created that I knew of was in my CD case on my tour bus.

When Tupac died, the world lost an icon. A soldier. A poet. I lost an idol.

I was grateful to have Afeni give me the chance to work with his a cappellas. I remember talking to her for the first time. It was a little nerve-wracking. I didn't know what to expect. I was about to talk to a woman who is a legend herself and her son is a legend. But the fact that Afeni gave me a chance to get his a cappellas and make beats around them and make an entire album with Tupac is one of the things I find just incredible. Every time I would make a beat around one of his a cappellas I would just pray I was doing him justice and that he would be looking down like, "Yeah that's the shit, Em, that's the shit. I like that . . . I like that."

Plaque from Afeni Shakur thanking Eminem for his work on the platinum album *Loyal to the Game*.

YOUNG DRE THE TRUTH

> Ex-gangbanger and recording artist Young Dre The Truth admired Tupac's lyrics, and used them as motivation to change his life. Later, he met Tupac and spent time in the studio with him, eventually earning an endorsement of his talent.

I'm from the east side of South Central. Tupac's music targeted me and my people. It was like Pac was speaking directly to us.

When he came out with "Death Around the Corner" and "Papa'z Song," a lot of us didn't have dads, and a lot of us really did feel death around the corner. A lot of us felt like we were "heavy in the game." I was riding with a Glock with thirty-six rounds in the clip, in a Monte Carlo SS with four gold Daytons. We were all out there, involved in narcotics and making money off it. It was just the only way for me I could see at that time. When you come up out of a black community, you only got a few choices: to either graduate from high school, which few of us did—I didn't—or get a nine-to-five, or go to college and play some type of sport, sell dope, or rap. And being a rap artist wasn't a choice on the list until the '90s. In the late '90s, rap became the top choice. Everybody was like, "Fuck school, I'm gonna rap." Or, "I'm gonna sell dope and rap." Or, "I'm gonna be a pimp and rap."

I was born in the game. I didn't know anything square. When Pac said in one of his songs, "My family consists of drug dealers, thugs, and killers," that was my life. I felt what he was saying because my cousins and my family are in the penitentiary. Practically everyone I know, even my mother, has gone to jail and done time. So when we heard him speaking on these things, we felt directly connected. Everybody can rap about cars and bitches. But when Tupac talked about some pain that somebody is going through, he was talking directly to me. When he'd say stuff like, "Ask me if I cried when the Pope died?" I could relate, 'cause no, I didn't. Our community cried when *Malcolm X* died. He would rap on things, and you would say, "This nigga knows how I feel."

Tupac gave you a different perspective. He made you understand you could have goals to get out of any situation. I was a nigga who was gangbangin' and got out of it. "Death

Around the Corner" was my song. It made me look at my life and learn from my mistakes. It made me look at my life and say, "I got to get the fuck out. I may not be done completely with this lifestyle, but I have to fight harder to know that I can make it. Look at Tupac. He did it." Pac's music was a lifeline for me that made me want to live. That was how he affected me before I met him.

I was affected by him in a whole different way once we met. I went to a Jack the Rapper convention in '93 and saw Pac there. He was in the lobby and he was talking to the heavy-set girl from Arrested Development. It was really crowded, and I got bumped by someone. And I was like, "Who the fuck is bumping me, what the fuck?" He had a black bandana tied over his face—outlaw style—so you could only see his eyes and eyebrows. The second I saw the "Thug Life" jacket, I knew who it was. I wanted to jump into his conversation and say, "Pac—what up?" But I didn't, because I didn't want to be rude.

The next day I saw him again. I yelled "Pac!" and he was like, "What up?" I tried to hand him a cassette with some of my music on it. I said, "Man, I got heat. You gotta hear this." He was like, "Homey, I got so many tapes." He grabbed his pockets. He had these purple sweatpants on, so his pockets were deep, and he had to have damn near twelve tapes in his pockets. I was like, "Fuck that, you gotta hear this." So after a second, he saw that I wasn't going anywhere and he saw that I was persistent. He took the tape and told me what room they were all staying in. There were so many artists at the convention: Kurupt and Snoop and Naughty by Nature. But once I talked to Pac, I was done. He was all I needed to talk to because it was his shit that I loved the most.

When I went to their room later, they were blowin', they gave me drinks, and kicked it. It wasn't like he was all on me, but he just accepted me in. I met E-40 and Mike Mosely, and that was the start of it all.

I started going to the Bay more after that because it was really the mecca of music back then. And I had always loved what Mike Mosely did with E-40 and C-BO, plus I was liking all the mob music sound. Pac, at that time, was working a lot with E-40, so that enabled me to be around him. One time we all ended up down in L.A. to record this track off of E-40's album. The song was called "Dusted 'n' Disgusted." I remember the day so clearly. Richie Rich was there, callin' Pac "the little African" all day long. Mike Mosely, Richie, Pac, Havoc, E-40, J-slip, Spice 1—everyone was there. I was trippin' because I was like, "I'm around Pac right now." It was just big shit to be in the studio with him. Pac had about two zips of chronic. E-40 had us on this Snapple with brandy. Pac was rollin' blunts in cigars. I had never smoked blunts that big. We were blowin', back to back. We were so fucked up in there.

That was one of the only times I got to watch Pac do his vocals. He wrote his verse in ten minutes, and then went in there and laid it in two or three takes at the most. Then he went over his doubles all the way like a lead track. Then he went over it again to make it extra thick. Then he came out of the booth and everyone was shocked. He had everyone amazed, 'cause he'd done the whole thing in like ten or fifteen minutes. Watching him do vocals was like being a student and a peer at the same time.

There was one point during the day that everyone started freestylin'. Pac kicked a verse. Then Richie Rich kicked one. It was like a ten to fifteen minute freestyle session. Then it went around again to everybody, but the next time they skipped me. I was like, "Damn, hold the fuck up." So when it came around to me again, I just got up and ripped that muthafucka. Pac was like, "Nigga, damn, you dope." E-40 was like, "You ain't gotta be so loud, cousin." I just wanted to be heard so bad at the time, so I was two or three times louder than everybody else. That was all I needed: for Pac to say, "Nigga, that was dope."

After the freestyle session, Pac was like, "Yo, what you got up man?" I told him that I was recording my album and asked him if he wanted to get on it. He was just so humble and cool, and he gave me his number again. I remember I was so excited that day, that he was about to be on *my* album. Waiting for it to happen was like waiting for Christmas. To be co-signed by Pac was like a boost of double energy for me. It gave me hope. It made me know that I could succeed in this music game.

> Although the two never had the chance to collaborate on any of Young Dre The Truth's projects, he was featured on Tupac's 2007 album, *Pac's Life*.

Backstage pass for the convention where Young Dre and Tupac met.

LAUREN LAZIN

> Although the two never met face-to-face, the documentary *Tupac: Resurrection* took documentary filmmaker and award-winning MTV executive producer Lauren Lazin and Tupac to a place where many in the entertainment industry spend an entire career trying to get—to the Academy Awards.

Though I never met Tupac, I had certainly been aware of him as an artist, especially when I was at MTV. He just dominated every story, every piece we did. I had directed a documentary on Dr. Dre, a show on Death Row Records, and a show on Snoop, and Tupac was often in the footage. It was as if a light was shining on him; you'd always think, "Look at him; oh, he's so interesting," or "Oh, he's so smart." He just *popped* no matter who or what you were doing a film on. If Tupac was anywhere in it, he was always right *there*.

When the idea of doing a documentary on Tupac came up, I really wanted to direct it. He was just so charismatic, so interesting. And Afeni is a very magnetic personality herself. I knew that working with her and on this project for the next two years would be something I would grow from as a person. Plus, I could see from the MTV end of it how much of a huge impact he had on our audience, and how much they loved him. And there was a whole new generation of young people who were buying his albums, who were absorbing anything that mentioned him. It was also really fascinating to me as a sociologist to ask, why is this particular person resonating with this new generation? They weren't even old enough to buy his music when he was alive, and yet he still speaks to them in a very profound way. So a lot of the making of the film was an exploration of what is so magical about him.

The way that we all decided to do the film was to get out of the way and let him tell the story. The first thing we did was gather all the information on him that we could. So many people said to me that you can really never know Tupac; he's very complex and there are so many different sides to him. Everybody I interviewed—and I did a *lot* of interviews—told of different sides of him that they experienced. So it was very important to me that the movie reflect and celebrate that complexity.

One of the things that really gratified me when the film came out was how many different kinds of people saw the film and related to it. I remember at Sundance some of the young hip-hop guys were there. That was great, because they were the people who were there for Tupac all along. But then these much older, conservative white guys came up to me after the screenings and said, "Oh I totally relate to him. I totally get him." Just so many different kinds of people relate to him, which is an extraordinary gift.

When *Tupac: Resurrection* got nominated for an Academy Award, I remember feeling like Pac should be there. I remember at one point being at this Academy Awards brunch and there was sort of this nexus of all these really excited black actors, like Jamie Foxx and Don Cheadle, and I just remember standing there thinking, *I shouldn't be here; it should be Tupac. This is the exact moment that Tupac should be right here, with these guys.*

Sundance was the first time the movie crew saw the film with an audience. We had just finished it. We had no idea if it would play on a big screen. We had no idea if it would resonate. It wasn't like we were going to a hip-hop festival where everybody would already be interested in him. But it played really, really well there each time it showed, and that was exciting. It's hard for one person to sustain a film for ninety minutes. You get tired of hearing someone's voice. But you don't with *Tupac: Resurrection*. Tupac could sustain the ninety minutes. His voice, his thoughts, his ideas, could sustain it. And he is big enough to fill the room. He filled that theater. He filled the room and he held it. There are very few people who could do that.

SHA MONEY XL

> As co-founder of G-Unit Records, Sha Money XL is responsible for bringing rapper 50 Cent to the mainstream. He has produced singles for artists such as 50 Cent, Snoop Dogg, Busta Rhymes, and Tupac.

I never got to meet Tupac, but one time I was in Jamaica Queens on Jamaica Avenue at this car wash, and I was a car away from him and Stretch. This is the time back when Stretch used to hang out with Tupac, and he'd be running through Queens from White Castle to Springfield and all over. Stretch had this green MPV. And Stretch, in my hood, was straight up gangster—so when you seen him, it was like, "straighten up." It was one of those car washes that you have to stay in the car all the way through. So I'm in my car already in the car wash and this green MPV pulls behind me. I'm a little dude and I looked in my rearview and I see these wild dudes in the MPV, smoke comin' out of it. Tupac's aura had me frozen. I was right in front of them, but I didn't do the fan stuff and run out. I was timid. Stretch had that presence in my hood where he wasn't approachable like that. Plus, I was younger so I was like, "wow, no."

I actually saw Tupac first as an actor. I saw him in *Juice* as Bishop and then "Brenda's Got a Baby" came out and I was thinking, "He raps too?" That was it for me. I was like, "He raps and he acts? He's ill . . . he's winnin'." Tupac was authentic; he was real. There was nothing fake about him. That is why he was able to capture so many different audiences. I don't believe that Pac had peaked yet. There was going to be a whole 'nother calling and a demand for what he would be doing. I think that he would've started producing. If he was here, he'd be back in New York recruiting every real nigga. That East vs. West shit would've been dead. He'd have the illest movie company, he'd have the best record label, he'd have been putting people's books out, he'd have been an enterprise.

You got rappers where you hear them ten years ago and it feels like ten years ago. I say ten years ago, because it's been that many years since he died. Some of his songs are thirteen, fourteen, almost fifteen years old. His vocal tone changed a bit in certain songs, but that makes it prophetic—what he's talking about is so current. He sounds better than the guys rappin' now. He doesn't sound little. He sounds powerful. When you hear some of the rappers still out now, back in the day they sound like little kittens. Pac growls. There was conviction and power in his voice that dated and cut through all this time and put him in the present day. The words add up to what's going on right now.

He was a prophet. Straight up. He gave a message. You listen to his words and the things he's saying. Some things are negative, but even though it's negative, it's gonna talk to that dude in the hood that needed to hear it: "Nigga, get out and git something," he'll tell you to motivate you. "Nigga, what? I'm back up and just came from jail—it's me against the world." It motivates a thug to go get it.

Tupac is the one who showed me that you gotta be true to who you are. Whether you're on the "fuck the world" shit or whatever you're on, be on it, don't get wishy-washy. There was nothing fake about it. He is a revolutionary. He stuck to who he was. He never came back and said sorry. He never came back and said, "I didn't mean that." He never had to.

I don't feel like it was an innocent thug who killed Tupac. I feel that someone saw something that they didn't want to see. I believe he was killed because they felt like he was the one.

THE OUTLAWZ

> Tupac named his protégés, the Outlawz, after so-called enemies of America. Kastro, his first cousin; E.D.I.; and Kadafi grew up with Tupac. Napoleon, Fatal, and Young Noble met him through Kadafi later in their lives. Kadafi was killed two months after Tupac died, on the day of Tupac's Atlanta memorial.

KASTRO

Because we're cousins, Tupac and I used to be at each other's place a lot when we were little. We used to watch all the shows that used to come on channel five on Saturday—*Fame*, *The A-Team*, and all the Bruce Lee movies. We would act the shows out. We used to listen to music all day long, especially New Edition and the Jets.

Then we all moved to White Plains. He had a paper route. He didn't have a bike or anything. He would just walk around and deliver the papers. He did that until he, Set, and Fe moved to Baltimore. I never knew Tupac was a rapper until he came back to New York from Baltimore to visit us. He was into L.L. Cool J back then. He'd come with his friend Mouse, his beat-box man. He and his man would be beat-boxin', they'd be rockin' it. He liked Eric B and Rakim, but it was L.L. that he was really trying to be like a little.

When Pac died, the world lost something special. As his family, we knew what he was gonna do with himself and what was to come. What he planned never came to fruition on a worldly level. In our little universe it did, but on a worldly level it didn't.

When Malcolm X was young, he was a knucklehead, and Muhammad Ali, too. The masses hated Ali, but now he's the greatest athlete ever and is honored at every historical sporting event. Hollywood made movies honoring both Malcolm X and Muhammad Ali. This is what would've happened with Pac. He never got the chance for us to say, "when he was young, he used to be a knucklehead."

He was so magnetic and sincere with everything. He was just that person. How could you not wanna be around him and not wanna be involved with what he was doing?

E.D.I.

I remember getting up in the morning to get ready for school when I lived with Glo and Afeni. Pac was always the leader. He would get us up in the morning and everybody would get dressed. Nobody was doin' anything for us. I was lovin' that because at my home, you know, I'm eight years old and my mother's doing everything for me. She's ironing my clothes, she's hooking me up with some breakfast. But at [my aunt] Glo and Afeni's house, I had to iron my own stuff, and if I was hungry, I had to get up early enough to catch breakfast, while there's still something left. It was like a lesson in independence. I liked that as a kid.

Tupac and I were in Mr. Lincoln's class together at the Lower Eastside School. The school ran into financial problems and they ended up firing Mr. Lincoln. Tupac organized a boycott at the school to get his job reinstated. We were in elementary school and this dude is organizing boycotts and you wonder why people thought he was too militant? My mother and Glo and Fe liked Mr. Lincoln, so they asked him to keep teaching us. He ended up teaching us in his apartment, and he kept all of us in check. We used to get mad because he'd knock us on our head, not hard, but he'd get us when we messed up.

We used to get on the train ourselves when we were that young and just run around and act crazy. We used to go on the weekends to see karate movies and stay there all day. Pac would come out of the movies and swear he knew every karate move. He just knew he was the expert. And then when someone else tried to do it, he'd be like, "Naw, that ain't how they did it. They did it like this." And he'd do his moves. He also used to make us play "The A-Team." I was Mr. T and Pac would always have to be Hannibal. He was always the leader. Every time we did something, Pac would be like, "I love when a good plan comes together," like Hannibal used to say. Those times remind me of all our kids now. I see Tupac in my son Malik, and it trips me out.

I remember one time my pops came to see me when I was living with Pac. And he brought me in the bathroom and he and I had this father-son conversation. He's runnin' his spiel about where he wants me to go in life and everything. After he finished rattlin' on, he gives me $5. So I'm The Man now with the other kids, 'cause I got $5. And the first ones I wanted to tell were Katari and Pac. And I'm like, "Yo, my daddy gave me $5." So Pac said, "Gimme that! I know how to spend it. Give me that." He took the money and said, "Let's go and get some candies." He just took it. I didn't even care, 'cause I felt like I did something good for the team with that $5. I might have ended up with *maybe* two pieces of candy. Tupac always had to be in charge; that part of him never changed.

NAPOLEON

I met Tupac when I was about fifteen years old. He came to New York around the time that *2Pacalypse Now* came out. He had heard my story, about my mother and father being killed.

Pac was real sensitive to people who don't have parents or have had to go through hard childhoods, so we clicked automatically. He was like, "let me hear you rhyme." My music was actually real gangster back then. I had a demo song called "Money and Murder," like all the stuff that I was seeing in Jersey, and Pac loved it. He said this type would fit right in. He was like, "I'm gonna holler at you." And we kicked it for a couple hours. He left and I kept in touch. When I got kicked out of high school, Pac and everyone else told me to fly down to Atlanta. I knew if I didn't go, I would've ended up getting caught up in the streets. I decided to go and it was on from that moment on.

I remember the first song we did together was called "Killing Fields." When Pac heard it over the phone, he cried. He said he was literally crying. And he liked the combination of all of us together and said he liked how I fit. That was when he said, "I want you in the group." At that time, we were not the Outlawz yet, we were Dramacydal. When he was in jail, he decided to call us Young Thugs. That's when *Me Against the World* came out and when we was called the Young Thugs on it. The first album we did as Dramacydal

Napoleon and Kastro (kneeling) with Tupac at a video shoot.

never came out; we had done it with Interscope, and before it was ever released, Pac went to Death Row. When he was still in jail, he changed our name from the Young Thugs to the Outlaw Immortalz. That's the same time he named us after the so-called tyrants of America: Napoleon, Kadafi, Hussein, Edie Amin, Fidel Castro, Mussolini, and Khomeini.

After he got out of jail, we all lived out in California. We lived at the Oakwoods and we used to go back and forth to Pac's house in Calabasas, but we preferred to be at the Oakwoods. When we were there, we always used to party, smoke, and drink and have girls over. Pac would always try to get us to grow up. At that time, we didn't want to. We was young cats back then. Pac was teaching us a lot. We were just little boys and he wanted us to be grown.

In '96, I flew out to New York with Pac and did the MTV awards. I remember after the party that night, Suge wanted to wait for the limos. Pac said, "I ain't got time to wait for no limos, I'm about to start walking." Pac always wanted to stay moving. So we all started following him through the streets of New York, and all of a sudden I see him giving out $100 bills to homeless people. There was a big crowd of people following him. A lot of people was giving him a lot of love, like "welcome back, Pac." This happened about a week before he died; it was like he was getting a last chance to walk with all of them. He gave a lot of love out that night. He gave out at least $2,000, man, just to anybody who looked like they needed it, just giving out money. It was like he was saying good-bye.

FATAL

I first met Tupac when he was in jail at Clinton Correctional Facility. He had heard about me from Kadafi, and how we were cool growing up in the hood. Kadafi was younger than me, so I used to look out for him. Tupac told me when he got out, he was gonna fly us to California. As soon as he got out, we flew out to meet him just like he said. For the first couple days out in California, I was just sitting back and observing everything, trying to figure out who else I was gonna have to deal with besides Pac. I didn't open up for about a month. Once I did, I got to know him and we started talking and it was cool.

He has many different personalities, so you really didn't know him when you thought you did. We'd be driving with Pac, going to different clubs, all the parties, and a lot of times we wouldn't have security with us. We would be out, and someone would come up to Pac and just start touching him and checkin' him out and he would just stand there. He wouldn't even acknowledge them. Later on he'd be like, "Why you all let that nigga get close to me? He could've had a razor. He could've cut my throat. Why you all let that

Tupac, Fatal, Napoleon (hanging), and Kastro.

Fatal, E.D.I., Tupac, and Kastro.

nigga get that close to me?" He'd be like wildin' out after he sat there all calm like it wasn't a problem. He would just do something to see what we would do or how we would react. He was really trying to see what kind of soldiers we were. I remember one time, days after this happened, we were in a club and somebody came and touched his chain. I came and grabbed the guy's hand backwards and started strangling him. And Pac was like, "Damn, Fatal, whatcha doin, man? Why you gonna kill the brotha? He was only checkin' out my chain!" So just when you thought you knew him, there was no way to get around him. He was always testing who you were.

When we did the song "Made Niggaz," Snoop and his boys were in the studio, and so were a couple other people. So everyone is doing his verse, and I'm quiet as hell, doing what I do. And when I get on the mic I sing: "We find excuses to loot, cock, and shoot/Blow the roof off them groups like Rock Mahd Rauf." I hadn't even finished the verse when Tupac ran in the booth and nearly tackled me and was like, "There's something wrong with you! There's something wrong with you! We can't say that!" The whole crowd was going crazy, and that's when they accepted me, and I knew I was a part of that shit. I was in the room with a bunch of celebrities and I was nobody—and after I did that verse everybody just acknowledged me and how good I could flow, and that felt good as hell. And Pac came in there and represented me like that.

I live in the worst part of America right now, in Jersey. And just on the strength of who I am, because I knew Tupac, I'm all right. To this day I can eat off the fact that people know that I knew Tupac. He changed a lot of people's lives, and I'm one of them.

YOUNG NOBLE

I've known Kadafi since the third grade and Fatal even longer than that. I first connected with Pac through both of them. They had always talked about Pac, but nobody in the hood ever believed Kadafi when he would say that his brother was a rapper. But when that *Source* Karl Kani advertisement came out with Kadafi and Tupac in it, I knew he wasn't lying. I was the first dude they called when they moved out to Cali after Pac got out of jail. Pac had got them apartments at the Oakwood. And they ended up taking me to Pac's crib on Wilshire. That's when I met him. He was fresh out of jail, paranoid than a muthafucka. At first he was like, "First and foremost, nice meeting you." But then he turned to Kadafi and Fatal and was like, "How you gonna bring somebody to the crib that I don't even know? No disrespect to you, Noble, but I'm fresh out and I don't know you and I don't trust nobody." We got past that, though, and he loved me to death.

First Tupac didn't know I could rap. Once I moved in with them at the Oakwood, it started off where I was gonna be a designer for the Outlaw clothing. He was just gonna help me get my life together. I was fresh off the block and he always used to see me draw and he was like, "You need to be the designer for our clothing line." I had been writing rhymes from when I woke up in the morning before I went to school, so I had like a hundred rhymes in this book. When I started kickin' some of them to Tupac, he was like, "You kind of good, man, for a beginner."

Tupac kind of got mad because he felt like I was hiding my talent. He said I was wasting everyone's time because it had been three months since I'd moved in. At the next meeting, Tupac was like, "Noble needs to be the last Outlaw. The last link."

Tupac was the most genuine dude I've known in my life. The most genuine, the most giving, and the hardest working. He was a young dude and he had a lot of responsibilities. I always think about how young he was when I knew him. He was only twenty-five, and he had so much on his shoulders. Sometimes I think, "Damn, I wish we were the dudes we are now back then." He used to be damn-near a father figure to us. We were young and dumb. Pac was the general. *All* of us were soldiers, but he was the general.

Pac was a Gemini. He would flip on you at any moment. One time Kadafi and I left the house to get some food from Boston Market. We were all supposed to go somewhere and when Pac got up and came downstairs to go, we weren't there. Once we got back to the house, he was like, "Ya'll leave in my truck with my money and went to go buy some food!?" He snatched our food out of our hands and threw it in the garbage. He took the keys to the truck. Two hours go by, and we're starving. Napoleon's little brother, Kamil, was making sandwiches for us and sneaking them upstairs. But what it came down to was that after all that yelling and throwing our food away, we didn't even go nowhere. So I guess Pac knew he overreacted. I think what it all came down to was that he really just wanted to cook for us. He took our food and threw it away just so he could cook all this food. He made chicken and all this shit for us. He was that kind of dude. I was like, what the hell is wrong with this dude? He went crazy on us for no reason, and then cooks for us. But dude had a lot on his brain and the slightest thing would make Pac snap. But it was all out of love. I was down with my big brotha for real. He's the only muthafucka I could ever owe something to besides the IRS. And I don't owe them shit, 'cause I paid them. I owe that man to try to be productive and be the best I could be. I owe Pac that for real.

ARVAND ELIHU

> Arvand Elihu was responsible for creating the very first university-level course on Tupac. His U.C. Berkeley class was titled "The Poetry and History of Tupac Shakur" and became a breeding ground for similar courses and symposiums at universities across the country, such as Harvard, University of Wyoming, and the University of Pennsylvania.

Tupac's raw talent as a poet is what primarily inspired me to start a class on him. When I first came to the University of California, I didn't really like to listen to rap music. I was strictly Bob Dylan and Eddie Veder. I was going through emotional times and I needed a change in my life—something not so gloomy, something with a bit more energy, something to lift me up as I adjusted to life away from home. My cousin told me to go get this CD, *All Eyez on Me*. After hearing "Only God Can Judge Me," I was blown away by Tupac's ability to create such clear imagery. I knew it was honest. Tupac's music was on a completely different level than anything that I had ever experienced.

At the same time I discovered *All Eyez on Me*, I was also studying medieval English history. We used all these primary sources in order to understand what people lived like back then, and I had this image of people sitting around a classroom 200 years from now and studying Tupac to get a clear understanding of the late twentieth century social environment. Tupac will be an invaluable tool for future historians looking back on and trying to understand our society.

It's been over ten years since I started the class at U.C. Berkeley. Since then I have received a degree in medicine from The Johns Hopkins University School of Medicine. I have completed my general surgery residency training at Loma Linda University. And to date, initiating and teaching the course on Tupac has been one of my most exciting accomplishments.

SONIA SANCHEZ

> Sonia Sanchez, a world-renowned poet, was heavily involved in the Civil Rights Movement and the Black Arts Movement. She met Tupac when he was just a baby and saw him grow to become a voice for his generation.

I've known Afeni Shakur for years, so I remember Pac as a baby. Something that's so important for us to understand is that Pac didn't get his sense of the world in some accidental fashion. He got it because his mother was quite political. His mother understood the world. She was in the Black Panther Party. She brought him a different way of looking at the world. It's not by chance that Pac could cut through class, color and gender, cultures, even age groups; his mother gave him that. In her politics and her organizing days as an activist, she dealt with everybody on planet earth.

My twins used to play a lot of loud rap music. I am not a revisionist; I would come in and say, "Please turn that down. I could hear all that music out on the streets." And my kids would turn around and say, "Mom, you just don't understand." Well, one day I came home and they were playing a piece loudly, and I came in through the living room and turned it down, then went into the kitchen to put some water on for tea. I turned to my kids and said, "Who is that, anyway? Who is that person?" And my son said, "Mom, that's Tupac Shakur." I said, "Tupac Shakur? That's Afeni's son." And I went into the living room and told the kids to turn it up. I stood there listening to him and I told them that that was brother Shakur—that was Afeni's son. They told me, "See? I told you all along that it was good music."

He had a most beautiful spirit. Every time he said a line, something resonated in your heart. His was a free spirit, a good spirit. He had contradictions, but I know of no person on this earth who doesn't have contradictions. The country would sometimes allow a person to come through years and years of contradictions. He was not allowed. I call him a prophet, in the sense that he was a young man who came telling the truth. Whether you liked it or not, he was gonna tell you the truth. His voice was a voice for the people who did not have a voice. The people loved him because he said what they were thinking, much in the same way that when Malcolm X came, he spoke the words that we were too afraid to speak.

"Love Poem (for Tupac)"

1.
we smell the
wounds hear the
red vowels
from your tongue.

the old ones
say we don't
die we are
just passing
through into
another space.

i say they
have tried to
cut out your
heart and eat
it slowly.

we stretch our
ears to hear
your blood young
warrior.

2.

where are your fathers?
i see your mothers gathering
around your wounds folding
your arms shutting your
eyes wrapping you in prayer

where are the fathers?
zootsuited eyes dancing
their days away.
what have they taught you
about power and peace.

where are the fathers
strutting their furlined
intellect bowing their
faces in the crotch
of academia and corporations
burying their tongues
in lunchtime pink
and black pussies
where are the fathers to teach
beyond stayinschooluse
acondomstrikewhilethe
iron'shotkeephopealive.
where have the fathers buried their voices?

3.

whose gold is carrying you home?
whose wealth is walking you through
this urban terror? whose greed
left you shipwrecked with golden
eyes starting in sudden death?

4.

you were in
a place hot
at the edge
of our minds.
you were in
a new world
a country
pushing with
blk corpses
distinct with
paleness and
it swallowed
you whole.

5.

i will not burp you up.
i hold you
close to my heart.

From *Like the Singing Coming off the Drums* by Sonia Sanchez.

CELINA NIXON

> When Celina Nixon found herself faced with the challenges of motherhood at the age of fifteen, instead of allowing society's negative label to pull her down, she let Tupac's legacy inspire her. She attended the camp run by the Tupac Amaru Shakur Foundation, and later started her career there. She was ultimately promoted to artistic director.

I had my daughter, Jeda Clark, when I was fifteen years old. All I could hear in my head about becoming pregnant at such a young age was, "Your life is over." I'm sure many teenagers believe the same thing, because that's what society teaches us, that we've made the biggest mistake of our lives and that success is over for you, all you're gonna be is a teenage mom and now you gotta stop your dreams. That was my first and only perspective. Tupac's legacy changed that for me, when I began to study his poetry and music. I think it was the fact that you could feel and know that he was so passionate about everything he was saying. And that it had a message. I think that's what drew me in as a fan when I was younger. It wasn't about any specific lyric, it was him. He was bigger than his music. I learned through his poetry and through his words and lyrics about who he was as a little boy, and I learned that we are all human and that we all make mistakes and that we've all sinned and that it's okay. I learned that people are gonna try to bring you down but that at the end of the day you have to be true to what you want to do and what you know is right in your heart.

The camp taught me that not only can I still achieve my dreams, but that my daughter was a blessing, not a burden. I can now help her develop her talents and teach her the things I've learned, and be a positive role model in her life without forgetting about myself and the things I want to do. Despite what people said, I still graduated at the top 10 percent of my class, still on time. The foundation really helped me with life-coaching skills, motivational speaking, and my career goals. When they asked me, "Where do you see yourself in ten years?," they truly wanted to know, and they really stuck with me. I put forth my best effort in life but also in the camp, trying to stand out so that I could possibly have a position in the future and show Ms. Shakur that I was really passionate about the program that she created to keep Tupac's legacy alive.

By the time I turned eighteen and was getting ready to graduate, Ms. Shakur offered me a position to assist the director. It was my first job out of high school. I was honored. I was in college part-time and working at the Foundation part-time. I continued to work my way up and I became the artistic director. Ultimately, I knew the vision and I knew where Ms. Shakur was trying to take the kids.

The best thing about this program is that you see students coming here with so many inhibitions. They are in a box. After they get through our program, you see the transformation. Once they're done with the final show that we put on, they are just elated, and excited and filled with self-confidence. They also have a circle of new friends and extended family within Pac's Kids. They are new people. Just as Tupac was exposed to the performing arts, so are Pac's Kids. Our students have an opportunity to learn about music and dance and self-expression, and they truly are changed by it and grow from it. They are able to look at life and opportunity from a new perspective.

When people ask me questions about working with the Foundation, it's something you can't really put into words. Because Tupac is so huge. You can almost ask anybody in the world who Tupac is and they know. The impact that the Foundation and the program had on me is huge because he's no longer here. Sometimes I think to myself, if he had not died, where would I be? I know it's an awkward thought, but it hits you like, wow, because of his death, look how many kids are being empowered by what he believes in, years later. This is what his legacy is all about.

If I were to have the chance to meet Tupac and sit down with him for a conversation, first I would cry really, really hard. I would thank him. I would let him know that none of his contributions to the world were in vain. That none of it went unheard. And I would let him know that we're still listening.

IMAGE CREDITS

Every effort has been made to trace copyright holders. If any unintended omissions have been made, becker&mayer! would be pleased to add appropriate acknowledgment in future editions.

Page 4: Amaru Entertainment, Inc.

Page 6: Static Free Films

Page 8: Static Free Films

Page 17: Amaru Entertainment, Inc.

Page 19: Amaru Entertainment, Inc.

Page 25: Static Free Films

Page 29: Amaru Entertainment, Inc.

Page 31: Jada Pinkett Smith

Page 37: Amaru Entertainment, Inc.

Page 38: Amaru Entertainment, Inc.

Page 43: Darrell Roary

Page 47: © Kathy Crawford

Page 53: Amaru Entertainment, Inc.

Page 55: Used courtesy of Lori Earl.
　　　All rights reserved.

Page 58: Alexandra Sovin

Page 59: Alexandra Sovin

Page 60: Alexandra Sovin

Page 69: Treach

Page 70: Rashad Smith for Dirty
　　　Jeans Records and Filmworks Inc.

Page 75: Amaru Entertainment, Inc.

Page 87: Amaru Entertainment, Inc.

Page 92: Big Syke

Page 95: Static Free Films

Page 96: Static Free Films

Page 105: Preston Holmes

Page 109: © Estate of Lisa N. Lopes (2008)

Page 111: © Mitchell Gerber/Corbis

Page 125: © Kathy Crawford

Page 129: Rick Griffiths

Page 138: Eminem

Page 139: Eminem

Page 141: Eminem/photograph of plaque
　　　by Jeremy Deputat

Page 144: Amaru Entertainment, Inc.

Page 151: Static Free Films

Page 153: Static Free Films

Page 154: Static Free Films

Page 164: Static Free Films

TEXT CREDITS

Page 45: *Vibe* magazine, September, 1996: quoted in Tupac Shakur fan Web site, 2Pac,
　　　Ernest Dickerson (Director of *Juice*) as interviewed by Andrea M. Duncan,
　　　http://www.geocities.com/Hollywood/Hills/5597/ernesttrib.htm.

Page 74: Academy of Achievement official Web site, Maya Angelou Interview, "America's
　　　Renaissance Woman," January 22, 1997, http://www.achievement.org/autodoc/page/ang0int-6.
　　　Reprinted by permission of the Helen Brann Agency, Inc.

Page 159-161: "Love Poem (for Tupac)" from *Like the Singing Coming off the Drums* by Sonia Sanchez.
　　　Copyright © 1998 by Sonia Sanchez. Reprinted by permission of Beacon Press, Boston.

■ **MAKAVELI** 𝕸 **BRANDED** ■

Official clothing line of Tupac Shakur. For more information, visit www.makaveli-branded.com.

ABOUT THE EDITORS

Molly Monjauze, a friend of Tupac's from when he was a student at Tamalpais High School, worked closely with him during his lifetime, and for over a decade has worked hand-in-hand with his mother, Afeni Shakur, at Amaru Entertainment on books, movies, and CDs.

Staci Robinson met Tupac through friends at Tamalpais High School. Staci has worked on several projects for the Estate of Tupac Shakur and has conducted over fifty interviews about Tupac since he was murdered. This is her second book. She is currently working on her new novel, *Beneath the Redwoods*.

Gloria Cox, Afeni Shakur's sister and Tupac's aunt, was a great influence throughout Tupac's life. She has consulted on countless Tupac projects throughout his posthumous career, including the Academy Award–nominated *Tupac: Resurrection*.

ACKNOWLEDGMENTS

As with every other project Amaru produces, there are a great many people to thank for their dedication helping to maintain and keep the legacy of my son honest and vibrant. Glo, Molly, and Staci, the book is quite beautiful, I thank you.

To each of you who shared memories of, private moments with, and in-depth thoughts of my son, I cannot tell you how much I appreciate your honesty, integrity, and generosity. This project has truly been blessed by your spirit. Thank you each and every one.

Special thanks to:

My husband, Dr. Gust D. Davis Jr., my daughter Sekyiwa Shakur, son-in-law Greg Jackson, and grandchildren Nzingha, Malik, Cameron, Miori, and Milan, my sister Gloria Cox, my nieces and nephews, my family and staff at the Tupac Amaru Shakur Center for the Arts, the Performing Arts Program, Amaru Entertainment, and my legal team, Dina LaPolt and Donald David.

This book was a huge undertaking, and could not have been done without help from the following individuals:

Aiyisha Obafemi-Mitchell, Alisha Takahashi, Amelia Riedler, Ashley Fox, Christina Paljusaj, Cliff Lovette, Constance Schwartz, Coy McKinney, Craig Rosen, Danielle Demerella, Dennis Dennehy, Derek Dudley, DProsper, Fairley McCaskill, Gary Greenberg,

George Pryce, Gobi, Heidy Vaquerano, Jada Pinkett Smith, Jamal Joseph, Jamie Cohen, Jasmine Guy, Jayson Jackson, Jenna Free, Jerome Peterson, Joann Bianchi, Joanna Price, Karolyn Ali, Karynne Tencer, Kathleen Cleaver, Kathy Crawford, Kenny Meiselas, Kristi Roehm, Lauren Lazin, Liza Joseph, Luke Burland, Marissa Wickliffe, Matt Greenberg, Megan Myers, Nahshon Craig, Naim Ali, Niles Kirchner, Paul Rothenberg, QD3, Rashad Smith, Rebekah Foster Ujima Sound, Rick Barlowe, Shayna Ian, Shenae Branch, Simone Reyes, Starbucks Pleasant Hill, Steven Vanucci, Tracy Danielle, Tracy Martin, Versa Manos, Wanda, Ron, Reigndrop Lopes, and Watani Tyehimba.

To Sandra Lee Johnson and Thomas W. Cox, who, even in their physical absence, continue to guide and protect us. We miss your presence and appreciate your spirit.

To all of the individuals who are listed in the image credits, thank you for your contribution to this special project.

—Afeni Shakur-Davis

Thanks to my son Carl Raheem, N.A., the entire Monjauze family, and Afeni Shakur-Davis.

—Molly Monjauze

Thanks to my husband, my babies Quincy and Jace, the entire Peterson-Robinson family, and Afeni Shakur-Davis.

—Staci Robinson

Thanks to my children, my grandchildren, Tre'mayne Maxie, and my sister Afeni— thank you for the opportunity.

—Gloria Cox

TUPAC AMARU SHAKUR CENTER for the ARTS

Your monetary contributions can assist the growth of the Tupac Amaru Shakur Center for the Arts. In addition, you can purchase a brick engraved with your company logo or personal message! Your brick will be constructed into the Peace Garden of the Tupac Amaru Shakur Center for the Arts.

ONE BRICK AT A TIME FUNDRAISER

Option 1: Red, White acre Greer, 4x8 - $100.00 (Placed in the Peace Garden)
Option 2: Blk & Gold, Marble Plaque, 8x8 - $1,000.00 (Placed on the "Wall of Respect")
All donations are tax deductible. ID# 582512839.

A portion of Amaru's proceeds from the sale of this book are being donated to the Tupac Amaru Shakur Center for the Arts.

All donations can be sent to:
Jeff Pitts at Spring Asset Management, c/o Tupac Amaru Building Fund,
17711 West Strack Drive, Spring, TX, 77379

visit www.2paclegacy.com and www.tasf.org for more information